MW00427565

In this book, Jonathan works hard to bridge the gap between our intellectual knowledge of God and our lived experience with God. And the result is a simple, practical, and powerful read with great tools for leading you toward a deeper, whole-hearted love of God.

—**Dhati Lewis**, lead pastor of Blueprint Church and vice president of the Send Network, North American Mission Board

Jonathan Parnell is one of the most thoughtful and interesting young writers in the evangelical world today. If you haven't yet read his writing, *Mercy for Today* is a great place to start. It is a theologically sturdy, pastorally sensitive, well-written devotional text. Highly recommended.

—**Bruce Riley Ashford**, provost and professor of Theology & Culture, Southeastern Baptist Theological Seminary

One of the most basic truths of Christianity is that we are always in God's presence. The challenge for many of us is to come awake to that reality. Of the many ways that I've been blessed by my friend Jonathan Parnell, this is at the top of the list—he helps me to feel the realness of Jesus. Whether it's pressing home the fact that I can actually praise God, or helping me to own the fact that my main problem is my distorted heart, or making me to feel the earnestness of David's prayer for God's presence, or reminding me that joy is at the center of the Christian life, Jonathan has a remarkable way of connecting God's truth and my experience so that I walk away with a greater sense that Jesus is real and God is merciful.

—**Joe Rigney**, assistant professor of Theology & Literature, Bethlehem College & Seminary, Minneapolis

A timely invitation to step away from ourselves, and who we think God is, to discover a deeper and richer mercy than we have imagined. This is a great little book to jumpstart a cold heart, and warm the affections for a greater God. Who doesn't need that?

—**Jonathan K. Dodson**, lead pastor of City Life Church, author of *Gospel-Centered Discipleship*, *Here in Spirit*, and *Our Good Crisis*

Jonathan Parnell offers a moving pastoral reflection on Psalm 51. The key to this prayer is that it is addressed to a God who is outside of us, radically other than us, but communicates himself to us by his saving presence. Parnell is after the "lived sense" of this reality. He invites us to appeal to this God for mercy, to thirst for our joyful experience of his presence. The oceans of God's mercy are more satisfying than the splash pads of self-justification.

—**Dr. Matthew LaPine**, pastor of Theological Development, lecturer, Salt Network School of Theology

God's pursuit of his people is relentless; his call to seek him is clear. The Christian's greatest joy is God himself. But oh how we falter in our pursuit while the God of mercy awaits us daily! Jonathan Parnell offers a clear, helpful path through Psalm 51 to daily seek the God who will be found.

—**Ming-Jinn Tong**, pastor for Neighborhood Outreach, Bethlehem Baptist Church

Mercy. It's not just something nice. It is the foundational need for every person on planet earth that, by God's amazing grace, realizes they are a sinner. Jonathan Parnell's book, based on Psalm 51, will once again open your eyes to this wonderful, necessary and not often talked about topic. Read the book! Allow God's mercy to utterly transform you!

—**Steve Treichler**, senior pastor, Hope Community Church, Minneapolis, MN

MERCY

FOR TODAY

— A Daily —

PRAYER

— from —

PSALM 51

JONATHAN PARNELL

B&H
PUBLISHING
NASHVILLE, TENNESSEE

To Melissa, my wife

ACKNOWLEDGMENTS

Paul asks, "What do I have that I did not receive?"—and I wonder, *What have I received that hasn't come through others?* My whole life is grace, and it's grace by means of people, and one of the best ways to cultivate gratitude, I've found, is to recognize those people. To acknowledge them before God, to give him thanks for them, and when it's possible, to thank them.

When it comes to this little book I'd like to mention a handful of people through whom God's grace has come, beginning with Bible translators. I read the Bible in English every day, and that's nothing short of a miracle. Though I preach from one English translation, I benefit from them all, and I'm grateful for every man and woman who has helped make that possible. To every translator and producer of any modern English Bible, thank you, really.

Thank you, Brandon Smith, for your early encouragements in this book, and thank you, Taylor Combs and team, for considering my proposal and moving forward. It has been a joy to work with B&H, and I'm especially grateful, Taylor, for your comments and help with my first draft. Thank you, pastors of Cities Church, for your encouragement toward my writing. Much of this book was written on Tuesday mornings when I didn't have a sermon the following Sunday, and that was from the blessing of these brothers. This team of pastors is the greatest thing I've ever been part of, and I love you, men—Aufenkamp, Easterwood, Foster, Kleiman, Mathis, Rigney, and Thiel.

Thank you, Matthew LaPine, for reading an earlier version of this manuscript, and for your help and encouragement. Thank you, Jon Fuehrer, for your blameless service at Cities Church (see 1 Tim. 3:10), and for your friendship. You have encouraged me more than you know. Thank you, John Piper, for your influence on my life, and for the ways you've encouraged me in preaching and writing.

Thank you, to my children, Elizabeth, Hannah, Micah, John Owen, Noah, Ava, Nathaniel, and you who are currently with your mother. You kids are more important to me than church folk, and I love you very much. God knows how rich you make me.

Thank you, Melissa, my wife and best friend, and the one to whom this project is dedicated. How in the world did this book make it here? How have we?

The mercy of God.

CONTENTS

INTRODUCTION

There are two things you should know before you read this little book: first, and most important, God is merciful; and second, because of God's mercy, our repentance is possible.

Right away I'm assuming this doesn't sound strange to you. If you're a Christian, you've heard before in one way or another that God is merciful. It's one of his most frequently cited virtues. In fact, I wonder if perhaps it's so frequently cited, right along with "grace," that we tend to yawn at the word. God's "mercy and grace" can become a blob category that we just use to say he's more nice than harsh. It can become our way of giving a respectful hat-tip, a creaturely nod of acknowledgment—but it no longer captivates us.

You know how this goes. Our overuse of deep words can tend to diminish our sense of wonder. We can reference realities with our mouths that our hearts can't grasp—partly because it's easier to polish our words than grow our affections. Indeed, this is one of the diciest things about being a pastor. I once heard it said that the most difficult part of pastoral ministry is that pastors must be close to God, or at least be good at *pretending* to be close to God. Oh my.

Am I truly close or am I pretending?

This is the kind of question that really matters to me, and it's in the foundational mix of why I've wanted to write about God's mercy. Pastors tend to *talk about God's mercy* at the conceptual level (I plan to do that in these pages), but we must also *testify of God's mercy* from our own experience (I plan to do that too). And though I'm writing as a pastor, I'm coming at this as plainly human. I'm as desperate for God's mercy as anybody who ever lived, and I'm going to talk and testify about God's mercy like that's true. My hope is that you freshly grasp the wonder of God's mercy in your own life.

HIS MERCY IS MORE

The mercy of God is a reality true to God's nature that we could not live without. Now, I realize we could say that about everything to do with God's nature; everything that is of God, pertaining to his identity, is indispensable. We don't get to shuffle the pieces and rank them. God is God, and he gives *himself* in all that he is. At the level of our existence, though, as fallen creatures who borrow every breath, God's mercy is the mystifying pathway of hope into everything else. I have breathed again, just now, and my heart is still beating—and I know about oxygen and organs and all that biologically enables me to stay alive—but beneath these ingredients and functions I am here in this moment *because of God's mercy*. And I mean that as deeply and truly as I can. If it weren't for God's mercy, I would not be here. You wouldn't either. We *are* because God *is* . . . *merciful*.

God is kind—that is what mercy means. Maybe you've heard it said before that God's grace is getting what you don't deserve, and

God's mercy is not getting what you do deserve. That's true, in one sense, and it will certainly preach, but it doesn't tell the whole story. God's mercy is more than that. Yes, it means pardon, and yes, it means God withholds judgment—but it all starts in the heart of God himself. In other words, God *shows* mercy because God *is* merciful. So we're not just talking about a thing God does, but who God is.

> If it weren't for God's mercy, I would not be here. You wouldn't either.

NOTHING HELD BACK

There is a special phrase in Luke's Gospel that speaks to these depths. It's found in Zechariah's prophecy in Luke chapter 1. Zechariah is prophesying about God's purpose for his son, John, and he says in verses 76–78:

> And you, child, will be called the prophet of the
> Most High; for you will go before the Lord to
> prepare his ways, to give knowledge of salvation to
> his people in the forgiveness of their sins, because
> of the tender mercy of our God.

Verse 78 is the third time *mercy* is used in the chapter. First, in verse 58, Elizabeth's pregnancy of John was understood as the Lord's "great mercy" to her. Then in verse 72, Zechariah called God's faithfulness to Israel "mercy promised to our fathers." Both of these mentions have to do with actions and things. The old, barren woman was pregnant with a child, and *that* was God's great mercy to her. It became as practical as a crying baby she thought she'd never have.

And also, many years before Zechariah and Elizabeth, God swore to Abraham that he'd do certain things for his people. He'd conquer their enemies and rescue them from trouble, and Zechariah summarizes all those things as God's "mercy promised." A surprising pregnancy and fulfilled promises—both are called *mercy*.

But in verse 78, it goes deeper. Salvation was coming for God's people, and the mission of John the Baptist was to make that known. He was preparing the way for Jesus by spelling out for folks how big a deal Jesus is. Jesus meant salvation. Jesus meant the forgiveness of sins. *But why?* What is behind even the sending of Jesus and his gospel?

> Verse 78: ". . . because of the tender mercy of our God."

Jesus has come because of God's "tender mercy"—that's the special phrase, and in the entire New Testament, it only shows up here. The word *tender* actually means "inward parts." It's referring to the stuff deep down on the inside, like how we might use the phrase "the bottom of my heart." We're talking about the place of profoundest motivation, and in Luke 1:78 that describes God's mercy. It is mercy as true and sincere as it possibly could be. There's nothing held back. This is ultra mercy—mercy extreme in its compassion. In fact, it's so unexpected and wondrous that we really can't wrap our heads around it. That's why Luke gives us images, first with a sunrise that overcomes the darkness,[1] and then with an

---

1. See Luke 1:78–79.

unforeseen neighbor who helps a man half-dead,[2] and then with a father who runs to embrace his estranged son who is timid with shame.[3] This is how the mercy of God looks. This is God's *tender mercy.*

BRIDGING THE GAP

At this point, though, mercy is still conceptual for us, even with our imaginations in overdrive. And while that is valid and important—*thank God for our imaginations*—something different happens when we begin to understand that we ourselves are in the same place as those people stuck in darkness, and as that man left for dead, and as that son who smelled like pigs rehearsing his lines on the long road home. That requires our imagination, too, but it's our imagination employed by the integration of truth and experience.

One counselor-friend of mine often says that Christians have a mental category for God's truth but a "learned sense" of God in everyday life. Sadly, those two are rarely the same, and bridging the gap between them is what the life of faith is all about. *Will I take God at his Word even when it's not clicking for me? Will I believe what God says over the other voices? Will I live like God is more real than my troubles?* Our faithful resolve to answer these questions in the affirmative becomes the most important strides throughout our Christian walk, especially when it means overcoming the hurdles of past wounds. It's not arbitrary that the apostle Paul uses the

---

2. See Luke 10:25–37.
3. See Luke 15:11–32.

metaphors of a footrace and a fight to describe enduring faith.[4] We must take the unchanging truths of God and wrestle them into personal relevance:

> *Yes, God is kind and merciful. He says so. He shows us in Scripture. I recognize this as truth. And I also know what it's like to be lost, to sit helpless, to feel shame. I know what it's like to need God's mercy.*

Connections like this shape our lived reality. It makes us see things differently. It is what we do when we pray.

BUILDING THE BRIDGE

There are already a hundred reasons to pray, and here's one more: prayer is the exercise of connecting God's truth to our experience. And I don't just mean the specific things we say in prayer, but the very act of prayer itself. Prayer, most basically, means *we come to God*. It means that we—you and I, people like us—approach God. *How marvelous is that?* We address God! Whether we're sitting in darkness (Ps. 88:6) or crying from the depths (Ps. 130:1) or resting in God's deliverance (Ps. 116:8–9), prayer is the act of speaking to God from our experience. It's when we actualize the truths about God we believe. It's the first and most important step of faith in lived reality.

This is the reason the psalms are so helpful.

When I was a kid in Sunday school, the book of Psalms was always the easiest book in the Bible to find. I had a teacher once tell

---

4. See 2 Timothy 4:7.

me that the psalms were right in the middle, and that if I ever wanted to read one I just needed to place my thumb halfway into the golden fore edge. It was almost like magic. "Hey, Mom, watch this." *Voilà!* The psalms. And it might as well have been magic—not how I could get there, but that the psalms really are in the middle.

In the earliest days of my disciple-ship I learned that the center of my Bible showed me how to pray. This book that was supposed to be a "lamp to my feet" (Ps. 119:105)—the verse quoted at my baptism as I exited the water—was a book that didn't just report truth, but modeled for me how to live truly. The Bible has never been a sterile collection of propositions, but more like a soundtrack to everyday life, and we get to sing along. Indeed, *we must sing along.* That's one way to talk about praying the psalms.

Prayer is the exercise of connecting God's truth to our experience.

HELPFUL AND GNARLY

God didn't us leave us to ourselves to figure out who he is, or how to come to him—and as we pray the psalms, we are learning both. We are learning to express, in real life, the truth we embrace. But it's not just truth about God, it's also truth about ourselves.

The Psalms show us that there is such a thing as *the way* of truth. God intends for us to live in congruence with his reality regardless of our circumstances, but the problem is that this isn't easy—and the angst is clear. We're only three psalms into the book before David is working through the difficulty of a good night's sleep. David penned the psalm after he had been chased out of

Jerusalem by an army of conspirators. There was a growing mob of men who wanted his head, and David was looking for a pillow. His enemies were chasing him, and the man needed sleep:

> But you, O LORD, are a shield about me, my glory,
> and the lifter of my head. I cried aloud to the
> LORD, and he answered me from his holy hill.
> (Ps. 3:3–4)

David remembers that God is his shield, and that God hears his prayers—and so, *goodnight*.

The Psalms get much gnarlier than this, though. While the psalmists often display brazen faith in the midst of adversity, at other times they are just trying to find their way back to God. "O LORD, rebuke me not in your anger . . ." (Ps. 6:1). "For your name's sake, O LORD, pardon my guilt . . ." (Ps. 25:11). "I confess my iniquity; I am sorry for my sin" (Ps. 38:18). "If you, O LORD, should mark iniquities, O Lord, who could stand? But with you there is forgiveness, that you may be feared" (Ps. 130:3–4). Most notably among these psalms of contrition is Psalm 51, which begins: "Have mercy on me, O God, according to your steadfast love; according to your abundant mercy blot out my transgressions" (Ps. 51:1). This is the psalm behind the contents of this book.

Psalm 51 is the psalm *par excellence* when it comes to repentance, but its greater message is simply that repentance is possible. That's the second thing you need to know for this book you're holding now, right alongside God's mercy.

REAL REPENTANCE

It's no secret that the good news of Jesus includes the call to repentance. The Gospels show us right from the start that John the Baptist rocked the Israeli world with his stunningly straightforward "Repent, for the kingdom of heaven is at hand" (Matt. 3:2). The book of Acts only makes it clearer. The preaching of the apostles demanded their hearers to repent. Jesus Christ has come back from the dead, for crying out loud! *That means something.* It means, at the very least, that business as usual isn't going to work. If Jesus has really defeated sin and death, then you can't live as if he hasn't. The new creation has broken into this darkened world and now everything is different. For the apostles, then, every human who heard this news—and who hears it to this day—is confronted with a decision. The message of the gospel has always been a fork in the road, and the invitation, the command, has never changed: "Repent."[5]

Repent because it's possible. Whoever you are, wherever you're from, whatever path you're following, you can turn. You can stop. You can *decide to follow Jesus*, as the old song goes.

Now, there are depths of wonder when it comes to *how* that happens. Repentance doesn't mean you're pulling yourself up by your own bootstraps. Not at all. It is something that God grants[6]—something he gives, not something you achieve.[7] And at the same time, the fork is in *your road*. The invitation is for *you*—and not as a one-time sort of thing, but as an all-of-life sort of thing. The

5. See Acts 2:38; 3:19; 5:31; 8:22; 11:18; 14:15; 17:30; 20:21; 26:20.
6. See Acts 11:18; 2 Timothy 2:25.
7. See Ephesians 2:8–9.

Reformer Martin Luther said it best in the first of his Ninety-Five Theses: "When our lord and Master Jesus Christ said 'Repent,' he intended that the entire life of believers should be repentance."

When you choose to follow Jesus, you are born again—*born again to follow him*. And every day you continue down that path, that long obedience in the same direction,[8] putting off and putting on, crucifying the old self and giving life to the new self, saying "No" in order to say "Yes." That life—an "entire life" of repentance—requires much mercy. As you walk this road, you are walking deeper into the mercy of God. That's what this book is about.

---

8. Eugene Peterson, *A Long Obedience in the Same Direction* (Downers Grove, IL: IVP Press, 1980, 2000).

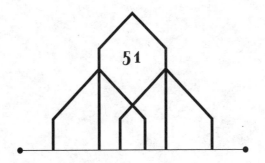

HAVE MERCY ON ME, O GOD,

ACCORDING TO YOUR STEADFAST LOVE;

ACCORDING TO YOUR ABUNDANT MERCY

BLOT OUT MY TRANSGRESSIONS.

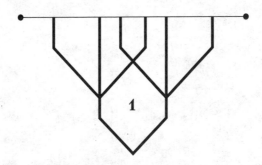

1

PEOPLE LIKE US

PSALM 51:1

Psalm 51 was in my back pocket, and I intended to keep it there.

By the end of high school, the psalm had been there so long, and through so many washes, that it's outline was practically embossed into the denim of my conscience. I don't remember whether I had heard the psalm from someone else or bumped into it while reading the Bible on a whim, but either way, I knew it came from a nasty situation. I had attended enough Sunday school to get that part right. And, of course, there is this dead giveaway before the first verse:

> TO THE CHOIRMASTER. A PSALM OF DAVID, WHEN
> NATHAN THE PROPHET WENT TO HIM, AFTER HE HAD
> GONE IN TO BATHSHEBA.

This is meant to be an uncomfortable psalm. It was so uncomfortable to me that, years ago, it hardly felt relevant. The only reason I didn't toss the psalm altogether was just in case I ever found myself in a terrible circumstance where I thought it'd come in handy. That's why I held onto it. That's why I kept it close—*in my back pocket.*

I didn't recall the psalm everyday, just when I did something really bad—like a high-handed sort of sin that wrecked my conscience and afflicted me with regret. Whenever I ended up there, in that gut-wrenching place, in that terrible circumstance, I'd reach for the psalm and quote it again:

> Have mercy on me, O God, according to your
> steadfast love; according to your abundant mercy
> blot out my transgressions. Wash me thoroughly
> from my iniquity, and cleanse me from my sin!
> (Ps. 51:1–2)

If God could forgive David, I figured, then God could forgive me. And since God expected me to forgive others seventy times seven, then there was no need to keep count of how many times I would ask it of him. This was my neat, logical arrangement, and I thought it was working.

THE STORY OF PSALM 51

Those superscript introductions we see atop the individual psalms—like the dead giveaway of Psalm 51—are meant to give readers a heads-up on the kind of psalm you're about to read. Sometimes the superscripts tie individual psalms together as larger sections, and other times they simply provide the biblical context in which the psalm was written. In the case of Psalm 51, the superscript does both.

Right away when we open the Bible to Psalm 51, we know we're looking at a "Psalm of David." That is one thing the superscript makes clear. If we've been paying attention to the superscripts of the previous psalms, we also know that it's been a while since we've heard from David. Book One of the Psalms (chapters 1–41), according to the superscripts, is loaded with psalms "of David," but the ones immediately preceding Psalm 51 are mostly from the sons of Korah (and then one from Asaph). Psalm 51 marks a return back to David that continues through Psalm 71,[1] and many of the superscripts found in this section include more than just the "of David" note. Unlike other places in the book of Psalms, these superscripts in Psalms 51–71 mention historical vignettes from David's life, with Psalm 51 being the most infamous.

The Backstory to Psalm 51

Psalm 51 goes back to 2 Samuel 12 when Nathan the prophet confronted King David. The writing of the psalm was occasioned by this confrontation, but the whole ordeal has to do with the terrible thing David did before Nathan got in his face. That is found in 2 Samuel 11. It had happened "in the spring of the year."

King David, who had been anointed king over Israel against all odds, was walking on the roof of his palace. That is how the story begins, and we're supposed to know right out of the gate that there is something off with this. We're told that springtime in Palestine was the time when the kings would go out to battle. But King

---

1. This means we count the "anonymous psalms" of Psalms 66, 67, and 71 as fitting within the pattern of psalms belonging to David.

David, at least in this instance, sent Joab and his servants to battle while he "remained at Jerusalem." David was in the wrong place at the wrong time.

The very first verse of chapter 11 tells us about this oddity, and while we shouldn't overdo the note, there is something to say about David sitting this one out, sitting at home, alone, doing whatever kings do when they sit at home alone.

David was raised as a shepherd. His father Jesse put a wooden staff in his hand, not a silver spoon in his mouth. David was at his best when he was on mission, focused, whether that meant killing lions to protect the sheep or leading an army to defeat his enemies. David had done both, and his impressive military triumphs are actually highlighted twice in 2 Samuel 8: "And the LORD gave victory to David wherever he went" (vv. 6, 14).

David, the scrappy kid brother of Jesse's sons who grew up watching sheep, had "made a name for himself" as king.

But this was the springtime, and David, for some inexplicable reason, was staying home. The text of Scripture tells us: "It happened, late one afternoon . . ." (v. 2).

Unthinkable Shame

King David saw a woman bathing. He saw her from a distance that late afternoon while he was walking on the roof of his house.

The story immediately gets embarrassing.

We're not given a great many details about exactly how all this happened—probably because it's too shameful—but David goes on to ask about who the woman is, the woman he had watched naked from a distance. He finds out her name is Bathsheba, and that she is the wife of one of his brightest soldiers. Then we're told that David "took her" and she became pregnant, and then after a failed attempt at deceiving her husband into thinking the child was his own, David arranged for her husband to be stranded in the field of battle, where he was killed by the enemy. Then David took Bathsheba, now a widow, to be his own wife.

In a matter of a few verses the whole thing goes from bad to worse to unthinkable. King David has committed horrible sins. It is sick and repulsive and inexcusable, no matter how you look at it. David, God's chosen king over God's chosen people, is called to be the model Israelite. He's meant to be the national exemplar in holiness and faith—the quintessential good guy—but instead has become the harshest of villains. Reputation recovery is impossible, and we modern readers should feel as incensed against him as we do against the men of power in our own day who are found out for similar crimes.[2] He is a scumbag. King David, this man whom men should emulate, this man whom women should trust, has perpetrated evil and tried to hide it.

But then comes Nathan the prophet.

The spokesman of God, Nathan, is the *gift* in this story. He is the embodiment of God's *grace* to David. He confronts him with a penetrating report about a powerful man who has murderously oppressed a poor man. Nathan says there was a rich man who had

---

2. David's primary sin, even worse than adultery and murder, is "the abuse of the office and position entrusted to him by God." See James Jordan, "Bathsheba: The Real Story," *Biblical Horizons*, No. 93 (1997). Accessed September 25, 2018, http://www.biblicalhorizons.com/biblical-horizons /no-93-bathsheba-the-real-story/.

an abundance of flocks and herds—too many to even keep track. There was also a poor man who had nothing but one little lamb—a lamb he loved so much that he'd feed it from his own plate and rock it to sleep at night.

Well, one day, some travelers came and needed something to eat, but the rich man refused to offer them something from his abundance; instead he stole the poor man's beloved lamb and cooked it to feed his guests.

Nathan barely finishes telling David the story before David's anger is "greatly kindled." Outraged by this atrocity, David declares that this rich man deserves to die for what he has done.

Then Nathan replies: "*You* are the man!" (2 Sam. 12:7, emphasis added).

Suddenly, it sinks in for David. And in a drastically shorter time than it took David to devise his sin, against all odds, *he repents.*

David says in 2 Samuel 12:13, "I have sinned against the LORD." And as the superscript of Psalm 51 tells us, David wrote Psalm 51 *in that repentance.*

MY BACKSTORY

David asks God to have mercy on him, and to blot out his transgressions, and to wash him thoroughly from his iniquity, and to cleanse him from his sins. And so I figured, as a teenage boy reading this psalm thousands of years later, that if God could do *that* for David, then God could certainly have mercy on me.

It wasn't hard to make this connection. I was a normal church kid growing up in the American South. I had a good family. I stayed out of trouble. I played sports and made decent grades. And on the rare occasions when I thought I sinned against God, or really, when I offended my conscience, I at least knew where to go. Psalm 51 was in my back pocket.

But the whole project, as I would come to see, was *religion* thick and *gospel* thin. My sin made me more superstitious than sorrowful, and my faith was borne more from convenience than actual conversion. It was no way to live, and so God intervened.

During my senior year of high school, I rolled my vehicle and sustained a traumatic brain injury. Pretty much everything I know about that wreck has been told to me. All I remember is waking up one day in the hospital, lying on my back with some shoulder pain and a dream-like daze. My first memory in this new world was seeing an eclectic bunch of faces gathered around my bed—my baseball coach, a pastor, my parents, and some unnamed medical professionals.

You crashed, they said, *and hit your head.*

Two small tears had ripped on the left side of my brain, and they had been bleeding. When my parents first rushed into the doors of the emergency department, they were greeted by a chaplain who had been waiting for them. Unless the bleeding stops, the doctors reported, the neurosurgeon would need to open me up and fix it. During that first night it was impossible to assess the full scope of the injury—*Would he survive? Would he walk again? Would he ever be the same?* No one knew. And so they all prayed.

Within a matter of hours, so I'm told, the tears sealed and the bleeding stopped (and my writing this sentence is living proof). When I finally regained consciousness, the gap in my memory felt like years. It had hardly been a day between the crash and when I opened my eyes to see the faces around me. I was still seventeen years old.

I came home from the hospital a couple days later and slowly recovered in the weeks that followed. There was no permanent damage. The whole thing was a miracle—there was no way around it. Photos of my mangled vehicle confirmed what people were telling me. I should not have been alive, but I was. I was very much alive, and my girlfriend was too. She had been riding in the passenger seat and had seen it all unfold in real-time. Apart from some cuts and scratches, her memory was unscathed. She had been among the faces praying for me to get well; and like with all the surprises surrounding this wreck, I would have never imagined that one day she'd be my wife and the mother of our seven children. It was a miracle, I'm telling you.

Locked Up and Buried

That wreck changed the course of my life. I had enough of a theological framework to understand that God had spared me, and that he must have spared me because he had a purpose for my life. One's senior year of high school is a time of big questions anyway. I had already been trying to figure out college and what I was going to do with adulthood. The wreck had humbled me and intensified the sort of things anyone my age would have been thinking about. Within the year, I knew I wanted to pursue Christian ministry, so I transferred to a small college where I could study the Bible with others who loved the Bible. It was in that study, during that discipleship, when I came to see I had Psalm 51 all wrong.

I didn't so much *understand* the psalm wrongly, but I had *used* it wrongly. David's prayer is a psalm for the guilt-ridden types who can't sleep at night. That is sure. The psalm is unmistakably a plea for God's mercy, based upon God's steadfast love. David's only hope for forgiveness is banking on God's heart, not his own. But see, I had *used* God's heart, and David's hope, as a trump card to throw down whenever I sinned. Understanding God's heart had not changed my own, it had just given me an "out" when I failed.

I realized that I had presumed upon the riches of God's kindness, and that it had turned me into stone. It wasn't long before I believed that a miracle greater than gashes sealing in my brain were the cracks forming in my hard heart. God moved me to deeper repentance, and it was during this time that I felt like I truly became a Christian. It was my "gospel awakening," you might call it, and it meant I had to change the way I went to Psalm 51. So I took it out of my back pocket and locked it in a safe. It had become a dirty psalm to me, and I thought that if I was serious about holiness, then I'd be better off pretending Psalm 51 didn't exist. So I buried the safe far out of sight and threw away the key, and it stayed there for more than a decade.

> Understanding God's heart had not changed my own, it had just given me an "out" when I failed.

I'd still bump into the psalm on occasion—at least annually when reading through the Bible. But every time I'd read it I always hoped in the back of my mind that I wouldn't ever *need* it again, not like I once did. I was convinced of God's mercy—*and I was changed by God's mercy*—but I never wanted to be in David's shoes. I wanted to keep my distance from Psalm 51.

Front and Center

One morning years later, during a time of Bible meditation and prayer, I found my way to a short daily devotion in *The Book of Common Prayer.* The devotion included a prayer of four petitions, each taken from the infamous Psalm 51. I was determined to stomach through this abbreviated form, and so, repeating David's original words, I simply prayed:

> *O Lord, open my lips, and my mouth will declare your praise. Create in me a clean heart, O God, and renew a right spirit within me. Cast me not away from your presence, and take not your Holy Spirit from me. Restore to me the joy of your salvation, and uphold me with a willing spirit.*

It was short and straightforward, and yet, to my surprise, God met me with a powerful experience of his mercy. Just like that, completely unexpected, I became convinced that this prayer was full of truth and relevance that *I* needed, not once or twice, but *again and again*. And so I went back and prayed it the next day, and then again the next day, and then the next day after that—and I haven't stopped praying it since.

In God's mysterious providence, I've found myself in a complete turnaround. This little four-petition prayer from Psalm 51 has become indispensable to me. It's the first thing I do every morning. It gives me footing for the rest of the day, and it's a lifeline in moments of chaos. I pray it for my soul and for my family, for my church and for my friends. This psalm that once seemed to me all about desperation, and then about shame, has now become a central part of my understanding of what it means to live the Christian life.

To be clear, I don't think there's any magic in the prayer itself. The good effect it's had on my soul hasn't just been in the fact that God is pleased to answer these petitions, but it's been in the ways the petitions themselves have shaped me. Prayer, of course, is about much more than just getting what you want. As Augustine has said, the words we use in prayer are not intended to instruct God, but to construct our own desires. That was Augustine's rationale for why Jesus taught us a formula for prayer in Matthew 6.

> As Augustine has said, the words we use in prayer are not intended to instruct God, but to construct our own desires.

God doesn't need us to inform him of what we need—Jesus makes this clear when he tells us "your Father knows what you need before you ask him" (Matt. 6:8). And yet, God still wants us to pray. In fact, it's actually *because* God knows our needs that Jesus tells us to pray a certain way—"Pray then like this" (Matt. 6:9). There are particular things God wants us to ask in prayer, and it's in that asking, in that constant remembering, that he works on us. So it's not "vain repetition" to sincerely ask God for the same things everyday. We tend to pray what we desire, and we desire what we love, and what we love makes us who we are. In this light, how do we not pray every chance we get, "Our Father in heaven, hallowed be your name"? These four petitions from Psalm 51, at least for me, are in that same category.

These petitions are worth repeating, fundamentally, because of *who* is doing the praying. Where I used to think Psalm 51 was more for the guilt-ridden types consumed with regret—a place I'd been before—I came to see that these petitions are actually for every human who knows they cannot make it without the mercy of God. As Eugene Peterson reminds us, prayer is, after all, "our most human action."[3]

And so if prayer itself is *that* human and *that* real, then what prayer could be the *most* human and *most* real other than a prayer for mercy?

What we read in Psalm 51, then, is not merely the prayer of a king who has messed up, but the prayer of a man who has fallen short of God's glory. This isn't so much the prayer "of David" as it is the prayer of a human, and that means a prayer for you and me, a prayer for people like us. As much as I didn't want to be like David, the truth is, at the human level, I am exactly like David and always will be. What he needed in his worst of moments is what I need all the time, because that's how it goes with God's mercy. And that's the point of these four petitions from Psalm 51. This prayer is about trusting God for the mercy we all need—mercy for today.

---

3. Eugene Peterson, *As Kingfishers Catch Fire: A Conversation on the Ways of God Formed by the Word of God* (Colorado Springs, CO: Multnomah, 2017), 59.

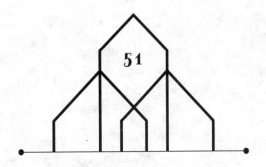

O LORD, OPEN MY LIPS,

AND MY MOUTH WILL DECLARE YOUR PRAISE.

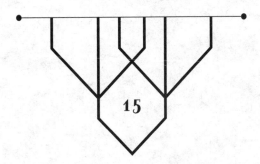

2

PRAISE

PSALM 51:15

"We are not good at this."

That might be the most honest approach we can take toward the psalms, and also the greatest argument for why we need them.

Eugene Peterson makes this case so well in his book *As Kingfishers Catch Fire*, a collection of sermons he preached during his twenty-nine years of pastoral ministry. Introducing his sermons from the psalms, Peterson explains: "Our habit is to talk about God, not to him. We love discussing God. The psalms resist these discussions. They are not provided to teach us *about* God but to train us in responding *to* him."[1]

That's why Peterson says, "We are not good at this"—even as natural as prayer comes to us humans.

And if we're not good at prayer in general, then we're especially not good at praise—not praise of God, anyway. We actually do

---

1. Eugene Peterson, *As Kingfishers Catch Fire* (New York, NY: Waterbrook, 2017), 61.

lots of praising when it comes to the things we enjoy, whether it's an exotic vacation or a sip of our favorite drink. Big or small, we tend to speak up about our pleasures, naturally inviting others to admire them with us. That's what praise *is*, C. S. Lewis reminds us, and it's basically involuntary, even for the plainest of people. In his *Reflections on the Psalms*, Lewis writes:

> The world rings with praise—lovers praising their mistresses, readers their favorite poet, walkers praising the countryside, players praising their favorite game—praise of weather, wines, dishes, actors, motors, horses, colleges, countries, historical personages, children, flowers, mountains, rare stamps, rare beetles, even sometimes politicians or scholars. . . . Except where intolerably adverse circumstances interfere, praise almost seems to be inner health made audible.[2]

Praise, then, is pretty much everywhere. If you take the wings of the morning and dwell in the uttermost parts of the world, wherever there are humans, there you'll find praise—and yet, why are we so bad at praising *God*?

How often do we come to God in prayer simply to praise him? When was the last time we knelt with the sole agenda of extolling his goodness? Why don't we brag on God as easily as we do our favorite pastimes?

---

2. C. S. Lewis, *Reflections on the Psalms* (New York, NY: HarperOne, 2017), 109–10.

It is fascinating, and noteworthy, that here in the West, among the greatest prosperity in the world, we're still more comfortable asking God to do something for us than we are recognizing what he's already done. We're better at seeking his intervention than at giving him adoration.

I'm not exactly sure why this is the case. Are we *that* distracted? *That* self-consumed? Maybe so—I have some ideas—but before we trek down that road of diagnosing our problem, it's best that we start with the reality of praise itself.

That's why verse 15 of Psalm 51 is the first petition of our prayer. It's the second to last petition in the psalm overall, but it's the first thing we're asking God to do in this prayer of a human: "O Lord, open my lips, and my mouth will declare your praise."

JOINING, NOT CREATING

"*Your* praise," David says. There is such a thing as praise that belongs to God, and David is asking to join that praise. His prayer is for participation, not creation, and there's a big difference between the two.

The praise of God, this petition implies, is something that has been happening long before David and will happen long after he's gone. We're all living proof of that. This past Sunday was living proof of that as my family gathered with our local church in worship. God was praised by a multitude of voices—and in St. Paul, Minnesota, of all places. And it was not up to me any more than

> God's praise resounds apart from us. That is one of the most wonderful things the Bible shows us.

29

it was up to David thousands of year ago. It is something that happens regardless of our little lives. God's praise resounds apart from us. That is one of the most wonderful things the Bible shows us.

Maybe the most compelling scene is found in Isaiah chapter 6.

THE PRAISE CONTINUES

By the time we get to Isaiah chapter 6, King Uzziah had died. That's the first thing we read before we are enraptured by Isaiah's vision. Uzziah had ruled for fifty-two years in Jerusalem, and it was fifty-two years of a relatively good reign, until he imploded with pride.[3]

Uzziah, as the story goes, had moseyed his way into the Lord's temple with a big-headed swagger. He wanted to burn incense on the altar, but according to God's law, the altar was the place of priests, not kings. But Uzziah didn't care. He broke God's commandments and despised his holiness so that by the time of Isaiah's vision in Isaiah 6, through the agony of leprosy and isolation, Uzziah was dead. The king had fallen hard, and he had become a warning for all who might take God too lightly.

That is the backdrop upon which Isaiah describes his vision.

Isaiah begins: "I saw the Lord sitting upon a throne, high and lifted up, and the train of his robe filled the temple." Isaiah didn't see God biting his nails, waiting for some human somewhere to praise him. God is not like a vain person pining for compliments,

---

3. See 2 Chronicles 26:16.

as Lewis once feared.[4] Instead, Isaiah saw God seated on his throne in all the grandeur and glory our imaginations can muster. The train of his robe filled the temple like smoke. Above him stood the seraphim—terrifying angelic creatures, each of which had six wings. With two wings they covered their faces; with two wings they covered their feet; with the last two wings they flew. And as

---

4. C. S. Lewis, *Reflections on the Psalms* (HarperOne), 108–10, Kindle edition: "The miserable idea that God should in any sense need, or crave for, our worship like a vain woman wanting compliments, or a vain author presenting his new books to people who never met or heard of him, is implicitly answered by the words 'If I be hungry I will not tell thee' (50:12). Even if such an absurd Deity could be conceived, He would hardly come to us, the lowest of rational creatures, to gratify His appetite. I don't want my dog to bark approval of my books. Now that I come to think of it, there are some humans whose enthusiastically favourable criticism would not much gratify me.

"But the most obvious fact about praise—whether of God or anything—strangely escaped me. I thought of it in terms of compliment, approval, or the giving of honour. I had never noticed that all enjoyment spontaneously overflows into praise unless (sometimes even if) shyness or the fear of boring others is deliberately brought in to check it. The world rings with praise—lovers praising their mistresses, readers their favourite poet, walkers praising the countryside, players praising their favourite game—praise of weather, wines, dishes, actors, motors, horses, colleges, countries, historical personages, children, flowers, mountains, rare stamps, rare beetles, even sometimes politicians or scholars. I had not noticed how the humblest, and at the same time most balanced and capacious, minds praised most, while the cranks, misfits, and malcontents praised least."

these modest, mighty creatures were flying inside this smoke-filled space, one called out to another:

> "Holy, holy, holy is the LORD of hosts;
> the whole earth is full of his glory!" (Isa. 6:3)

The creature's voice was so loud that the foundations of the temple began to shake, the smoke only grew thicker, and Isaiah never thought for a second that the reason God had recruited him there was because God *needed* worship.

In fact, Isaiah wasn't even compelled to sing along. Before he said anything he realized how out of place he was.

This wasn't like the concert of his favorite band. There was nothing about this spectacle that was sensitive to his being there. Instead, Isaiah was utterly exposed. In the light of such wonder he saw clearly where he stood:

> "Woe is me! For I am lost; for I am a man of
> unclean lips, and I dwell in the midst of a people of
> unclean lips; for my eyes have seen the King, the
> LORD of hosts!" (Isa. 6:5)

Isaiah had seen God, and he knew that what he had seen of God is true of God, whether he had seen it or not. God would be praised, and his praise would continue, with or without Isaiah.

David understands that same truth in Psalm 51.

THE GOD YOU CAN'T IMAGINE

The ceaseless praise of God we see in Isaiah 6, and that still exists in Psalm 51, is connected to a fundamental truth about God that often gets sidelined today. It's that God's reality is not diminished by our inability to comprehend him.

God is no less real because our grasp of him is elusive. He depends on nothing for his being, but instead all things are dependent upon him. That is why our praise can only be responsive and participatory but never creative. We have not invented him. God is the God you can't imagine.

This is very basic when it comes to God, and many of us would at least get this question right on a quiz. And yet, this is such an important truth to talk about because the world around us tells a different story. At the societal level, as part of the air we breathe,

> God's reality is not diminished by our inability to comprehend him.

people often try to shrink God down to a size that they can fit into their own heads. Of course, no one claims to be doing this, but that's what is happening any time you hear someone start a sentence with "I can't imagine a God who [fill in the blank]."

I've heard well-intentioned Christians say things like that, and even write books based upon that premise—but what is actually happening there? What is behind that kind of statement?

Those who think and speak that way are simply confining God to the limits of their own understanding. They are thinking of God only on their terms, according to the standards they find acceptable—*God can only be God if he stays within the bounds I've set,* the logic says.

This kind of thinking is rooted in pride—the pride of making God into one's own image, rather than submitting to the God who simply *is.* Not only is this wrong; it's also dangerous. It's the seedbed of bad theology and eventually apostasy. That's because the Bible relentlessly challenges any figment of God that people forge with their own minds, and to be honest, the whole thing is almost too predictable.

Eventually, if this kind of thinking persists, what the Bible says about God will not square with the limits we've set on him, which creates a subtle crisis. That crisis eventually leads to a game of exegetical Twister with the biblical text. We are forced to stretch and maneuver all we can to find a preferable interpretation of the text without toppling over. This sort of thing is too exhausting to be sustainable, so before long we give in. We start compromising the authority of Scripture, crediting our conscience with a voice deeper than the words of God. The more we do this over time, and sometimes sooner than later, we will just end up walking away from God completely.

This kind of apostasy is heart-breaking and misguided, and maybe the misguided part is the saddest of the whole thing. I've seen it before. The person thinks that walking away from God is brave and adventurous, that they're somehow embarking upon a newfound freedom. But really, they're not walking away from God at all; *they're just walking away from their own misunderstanding.* That's the terrible irony. People assume they're rejecting God, but they're actually rejecting their misconception of God. They're not free from God; they're enslaved to their own selves. They're abandoning the mess they've made with their own imaginations after hacking up the Bible and blending it with a cultural wish list.

Most people want a box-lunch version of God, a deity who is adequate but mobile, a deity who curbs my hunger but also fits into a small container I can carry wherever I want. But that's not who God is. It's doesn't work that way. God is the God you can't imagine.

TWO FRAMES ON OUR WORLD

It's also worth noting that we're more prone to think wrongly about God in our modern times than people did in centuries past. I don't mean heresies didn't exist in the past—of course they did—but today the mainstream way people conceive of religion is categorically different than how it used to be. It has to do with two opposing frameworks for how people understand reality. There is a *moral framework* and then there is a *psychological framework*.

When it comes to the moral framework, that's where we draw clear lines. There *is* such a thing as right and wrong. There *is* absolute truth. Reality *is* reality regardless of my own thoughts. The moral framework is the story from outside, the external word. But when it comes to the psychological framework, that's where the world is only what we're able to compute, where everything orbits around the self and our interpretation. The psychological framework is the story from the inside, the internal word.

In the moral framework, when it comes to theology, it is completely acceptable that God rubs us the wrong way sometimes. Certainly there will be things about him that we don't understand, or maybe even that we wouldn't prefer—*because God is God apart from us.* He's God. He is who he is. He is *holy, holy, holy,* as the seraphim put it, and we stand before *him.*

But in the psychological framework at its worst, God exists only for us, and therefore we will only want the parts of God that we find personally therapeutic. This is where near-sighted empathy reigns over time-tested truth.[5] It's where we only value the easily digestible portions of God, the box-lunch version, the kind packed with processed theology. This theology feigns being edgy and profound, but it's as tired as the golden calf. The real whirling adventure, as Chesterton said, is orthodoxy itself. There is nothing "so perilous and so exciting" as embracing the God who has revealed himself to us in Scripture.[6] That means holding together what he has made known and what he hasn't, and for us to settle for anything less is like choosing splash-pad entertainment over stepping into the ocean shoreline.

My wife and I are fans of splash pads. If you're not familiar with them, they're simply concrete slabs at parks or pavilions arranged to shoot, spray, and dump water for the amusement of kids. There are a handful of them throughout our city, and it's always the safest way to let our brood have a little water fun in the summer. They can get wet and splash around all they want, and we don't have to

5. See Joe Rigney, "The Enticing Sin of Empathy," Desiring God, http://www.desiringgod.org/articles/the-enticing-sin-of-empathy. Accessed May 31, 2019.
6. G. K. Chesterton, *Orthodoxy,* in *The Collected Works of G. K. Chesterton,* Vol. 1 (San Francisco, CA: Ignatius, 1996), 305–6.

worry about them going under. It might even mean we ourselves can relax, at least for a minute.

But the ocean shoreline is nothing like that. The currents that swirl on the beach are untamed, and the more we wade into those waters, the more carefully we must step. On the shoreline it never escapes you that you're staring into something bigger than yourself, something teeming with life you can't see, whose bounds are completely beyond your senses.

When it comes to the transcendent, because we often want the sensation of water without the ferocity of the waves, we tend to stick to the splash pads. Make-believe fun is safer than mystifying joy, after all. The same goes for the psychological framework where the self is more real than God, where our interior feels more legitimate than the exterior of God's reality. It is safer inside, but less true, and therefore the world of Psalm 51 will have none of it.

In the world of the Bible, the real world, God has given us a moral framework full of meaning and purpose regardless of whether we know it or not. Right now, in this very moment, even if you've never uttered a word of adoration to God, even if you didn't exist, the seraphim would still be doing what they do. The chorus would still resound: "Holy, holy, holy is the LORD of hosts; the whole earth is full of his glory!"

That is happening right now.

That's because God is the God you can't imagine, because he is the God outside of us, and he will be praised whether we're part of it or not.

THE "MY" THAT MATTERS

At the same time, while the praise of God exists apart from David, David still wants a part. That's why he prays: "O LORD, open *my* lips, and *my* mouth will declare your praise." Those are two possessive determiners that are very important. David is desiring to praise God as a person, as an individual. He wants to use the lips and the mouth God has given *him* to join in God's praise. And this brings us to a serious caution we must consider.

The caution is that we not completely erase ourselves from the picture. There is such a thing as overreaction. For example, we should be careful in our recognition of God's endless praise that we don't lose the gospel's claim on the individual. God's plan, indeed, has always been to save a people from all peoples. It is right to recover the gospel's corporate wonder. Jesus says "I will build my church" (Matt. 16:18), which means it's never been all about "me and God." We are not like two peas in a pod with the sovereign Ruler of the universe, and yet, at the same time, the Bible does tell us that God knows us and cares for us so much that he tracks the number of hairs on our heads (Matt. 10:30)—*that means each of our individual heads.* As individuals we are responsible for bearing our own load (Gal. 6:1–5), and for responding to the gospel with our own faith (Rom. 10:10–13), and for giving an account of ourselves to God (Rom. 14:12). There's a difference between our cultural individualism, and the Bible's high view of the individual. In our attempts to not be individual-*ized*, we must also not be individual-*less*. We must embrace God as neither centered on persons nor apathetic to them, but as genuinely *personal*.

God is the God you can't imagine. He is the God outside of us. And yet, we're still *here*, in this world, in the picture, and what we think about God matters. God made us, and he gave us mouths for a reason. There are lots of reasons, in fact, for why we have mouths, but the main reason, or at least the main reason in David's mind in Psalm 51:15, *is God's praise.*

This is why David asks God to use his mouth, and that's why we ask the same thing after David. We pray for God to open our lips so that our mouths declare God's praise *because we know that's the reason God has given us mouths.*

The psalms talk a lot about our mouths, and it always goes one of two ways. Either our mouths speak lies and are full of violence, or they speak truth and are full of praise—and a repeated prayer throughout the psalms is for the latter (emphasis added):

- Psalm 34:1—"I will bless the LORD at all times; *his praise shall continually be in my mouth.*"
- Psalm 71:8—*"My mouth is filled with your praise,* and with your glory all the day."
- Psalm 145:21—*"My mouth will speak the praise of the LORD,* and let all flesh bless his holy name forever and ever."

Our mouths are good for nothing greater than praising God. That's because praising God is the ultimate purpose for everything God has made—everything from seraphim to people like us. And so he commands us in Psalm 113:1,

> Praise the LORD! Praise, O servants of the LORD, praise the name of the LORD!

Everyday from now to forever, and every moment from the rising of the sun to its setting, the name of the Lord is to be praised. This is praise that is happening regardless of you and me, and yet God has given us these mouths. His praise is what these mouths are for—*it's what your mouth is for:*

You can literally *praise God.* You can actually lift your voice and sing along with the seraphim. *You* can sing with the seraphim. Think about that. You can sing and shout and speak of God, and not just *about* him, but *to* him. Over your sin, you can *declare* God's grace. Over your weakness, you can *declare* God's strength. Over the craziness of your circumstances and the sorrow of your sufferings and the darkness of your doubts, *your mouth can declare the truth of God.*

This is only so because God is the God we can't imagine, because his truth comes from outside of us.

LEADING WITH OUR MOUTHS

The implications here reach down into our most human experiences. Because God is God apart from us, even if we are not "there" psychologically, even if our emotions don't line up, even when it seems like everything in our lives is falling apart, our mouths can still join the chorus of God's adoration.

We can *say* true things without feeling them as long as we *want* to feel them. And if we don't know exactly what to say, we can simply take up the Bible and read. We can speak the praise of God in the Word of God. We can declare his praise with our mouths over and over again until our hearts catch up. In other words, *we can lead our hearts with our mouths.*

That's one of the ways we talk about it at our church, and only God knows how many times we must do that on Sunday mornings if we're going to sing at all. I mean that at least for myself. Each Sunday, about fifteen minutes or so before the start of our worship service, everyone involved in the service circles up to review the liturgy and pray. Several different pieces converge in that one moment. We have come to this gathering to *lead in worship*, not perform, and so it's for worship's sake that the band has rehearsed, and the exhorter, Scripture reader, and preacher have all prepared. Everybody has been working toward the same page, but that preservice huddle is the first moment everyone is together in person.

> We can *say* true things without feeling them as long as we *want* to feel them. And if we don't know exactly what to say, we can simply take up the Bible and read.

I'd like to say that those are always deep and meaningful moments, that everyone's heart is busting at the seams to lift Jesus high, and that we're bewildered by such an honor—but that's not how it feels a lot of the times, and not because we don't want it that way. A lot of the times as we gather together, some or most of us may just not be "there" yet.

Some of this comes with the territory of being a church plant and renting space, but for a while it seemed like every Sunday a wrench would get hurled into our plans. At one point we had worshipped in five different buildings over the course of a year, and too often we would rush into the time of pre-service prayer winded and stressed because something was off somewhere. This is not even to mention the internal struggles and pains we often carry as humans in a sinful world. And yet, there we were, gathered by the gospel, with our spastic emotions, about to lead God's people in worship. So we prayed. We prayed for a lot of things, of course, but we especially prayed for our hearts. We prayed *ahead of our hearts*. Those little prayers, while not profound by any means, stand as some of the most sincere prayers I've ever shared with other brothers and sisters . . .

> *Father, the sound keeps cracking; the floors are dirty again; the bathroom lights are broken; things are chaotic around here; distractions abound; and we praise you!*
>
> *We will praise you, Lord, from this time forth and forevermore. We will extol you among the peoples! Your steadfast love is great and your faithfulness endures forever—yes it does—and so we're going to sing; we're going to declare your truth; we're going to exalt Jesus. We're going to praise you. We want to praise you. Make us praise you.*

That is what it looks like to lead your heart with your mouth, and it's relevant for every worshipper of God as we come to the church's corporate gathering.

WHEN THE CHURCH WORSHIPS

God has patterned the world such that we can expect Sunday morning to show up at the exact same time each week, but that doesn't mean our hearts show up too. We might know where to go and what to do, but what if our emotions are left behind, perhaps buried under hardship or drained dry by loss? Sometimes our circumstances can feel so heavy that we can't imagine our hearts lifted in worship, and if the heart's not lifted, what's the point? Why should we bother with worship when everything around us feels so dark?

This is a real question, and God only knows the number of times it's been humbly asked by Christians in the midst of distressing circumstances, stuck in the miry bog. It is not a bad question.

We might think that the miry bog is the place of waiting, not worship. We might think that worship comes after the deliverance, and indeed, sometimes it does. In Psalm 40, David sings,

> I waited patiently for the LORD; he inclined to me
> and heard my cry. He drew me up from the pit of
> destruction, out of the miry bog, and set my feet
> upon a rock, making my steps secure. He put a new
> song in my mouth, a song of praise to our God.
> Many will see and fear, and put their trust in the
> LORD. (vv. 1–3)

Amen. God is able to rescue us from the pit, and we will sing his praise. Amen.

But that doesn't mean we sit out on his praise until the rescue comes. We can worship *in* the waiting. We can worship in the pit, neck deep in the bog, even smack-dab in the belly of a whale, or behind bars shackled by chains.

We know that Jonah was still figuring things out when he praised God from within the fish,[7] and I can't imagine that Paul and Silas were their emotional best when they sang hymns to God from the Philippian jail.[8] And yet, in both cases, from within their troubles, before their deliverance, they worshipped God. They opened their mouths, and they spoke truth. And so can you.

> *Father, my heart feels cold. My emotions are numb. I'm going to drown in this pit if you don't save me. Get me out of this, please. Rescue me, please. I'm flat-lining here, but you are still worthy of praise. Your word says, "Praise the LORD!" And I want to praise you, Father, I do—or I want to want to. Still, you say: "Praise the LORD from the heavens; praise him from the heights! Praise him, all his angels! Praise him, all his hosts! Praise him, sun and moon, praise him, all you shining stars!" (Ps. 148:1–4). All your creation gives you praise, so I'm going to praise you too. I will praise you, God. Make me praise you.*

WHATEVER COMES

Make me praise you. Isn't that David's prayer in verse 15 of Psalm 51? "Open my lips, and my mouth will declare your praise."

---

7. See Jonah 2:9.
8. See Acts 16:25–34.

This petition is pretty straightforward: *God, let me get in on your praise, come what may.*

That's the paraphrased way I've learned to pray this verse every morning.

Hours before we huddle in our preservice meetings on Sundays, before I really do anything on any day, I've picked up the little habit of repeating Psalm 51:15 just as it's found in Scripture. I quote it first, "Open my lips, and my mouth will declare your praise"—and then I cut to the chase: *Father, let me get in on your praise!*

It's the first thing I ask God after I rub the sleep from my eyes and get the coffee started. It's the petition to put all other petitions in their place. Although it's short and plain, over the years this little line has proven itself to be freighted with more wonder than I deserve to know.

That's because we never know when we wake up how our day will turn out. We have our schedules, our plans, our hopes—we can have all of that and more—but we can *never* have certainty about how the details will unfold. We are always stepping out into a mystery, into a world that exists apart from us. Only God knows what lies ahead—so what does that mean for you and me?

What can we do from this small place, from this perspective of ignorance, this humble shoreline as we stare into the vast ocean of God and his reality?

Well, because God is the God I can't imagine, the God who is God apart from me, and because this God has given me a mouth, I want to get out of my own head and I want to live in his truth. I want my mouth, my little self, to share in the greatest, most wondrous thing already happening in the universe, all day, every day.

I want God to make me do what I'm not good at. I want to declare God's praise.

————•————————————•————

Here I am again, Father, by your grace. You are the lifter of my head, and you've brought me here with lungs that breathe and a heart that beats, and this mouth that speaks. My God, I don't know all that's going to happen today. I just don't know. *But you know because you are God.* You are the God greater than I can imagine, the God who is God apart from me, and whose praise has never ceased, and never will. So whether or not I say another word, your praise is going to go on. You don't need my praise, but Father, would you let me praise you? Would you take these lips, this mouth, and would you draw me into that wondrous chorus of the seraphim? Make me lift my voice and speak the words of your truth, of your glory. Father, open my lips today, right now, please—open my lips, and my mouth will declare your praise. *Father, let me get in on your praise!* In the name of Jesus, amen.

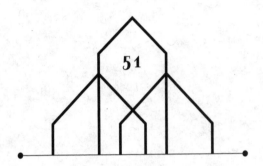

CREATE IN ME A CLEAN HEART, O GOD,

AND RENEW A RIGHT SPIRIT WITHIN ME.

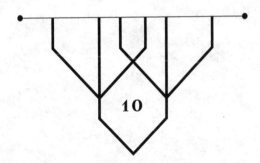

3

CHANGE

PSALM 51:10

Many years before David was idling on the rooftop of his palace, he stood humbly in the company of his older brothers, all seven of them bigger and stronger than he. This scene is one of the most profound moments in Israel's history. We read about it in 1 Samuel 16.

The prophet Samuel had been tasked by God to find a new king for his people. The first king, Saul, had been rejected by God, which is an important story all its own.[1] Saul defied the words of God, set up a monument for himself, and cared more about others' opinion of him than God's—so God tore the kingdom away from him. And the prophet Samuel grieved over this. The whole Israel-has-a-king thing was not working out.

By the opening of chapter 16, though, God had a new mission for his prophet. Samuel was to wipe his eyes over Saul and go to the

---

1. See 1 Samuel 15:1–31.

house of Jesse the Bethlehemite. Jesse had a house full of sons, and God had chosen one of those sons to be the next king.

When Samuel arrived in Bethlehem, the elders of the city weren't excited to see him. Apparently a reputation of judgment preceded this prophet—he wasn't exactly meek and mild.[2] But Samuel assured the elders that he had come peaceably and that he wanted to sacrifice to the Lord. He invited all the elders to join him, including Jesse and his sons. As each of the sons filed in line to the event, Samuel was anticipating the next king of Israel. He was waiting for God to show him "God's man."

First, there was Jesse's son Eliab, and Samuel just knew he must be the one. "Surely this is him," he thought, but the Lord said no and offered a vital correction: "Do not look on his appearance or on the height of his stature, because I have rejected him" (1 Sam. 16:7).

Apparently Eliab was tall and strong, just like King Saul had been.[3] Samuel was working with a one-dimensional category for this next king, but God explained that's not how this goes. *Don't look on the outside*, God said—

> For the LORD sees not as man sees: man looks on
> the outward appearance, but the LORD looks on the
> heart. (16:7)

So Jesse called the second son, Abinadab, but God said no again. Next came Shammah—a third no. Jesse kept trying, though, and eventually seven of his sons were standing before Samuel. God had said no to them all.

---

2. See 1 Samuel 15:33.
3. See 1 Samuel 9:2.

Samuel had to be a little confused by this point. God told Samuel the next king was a son of Jesse, but he had seen God reject seven of these sons in a row, and so he rightly wondered: "Jesse, is this all of them?"

Jesse replied, "There remains yet the youngest, but behold, he is keeping the sheep" (1 Sam. 16:11).

God knows how much I love this line. In short, Jesse answers Samuel's question with a "Yeah, sorta." He says: *All my sons are here; technically there's one more, but he's just the little guy out watching sheep.*

The Hebrew word translated "youngest" also means smallest. It carries the idea of insignificance, of being a nobody. We're talking about the proverbial little guy, but Samuel told Jesse to bring him anyway: "Send and get him, for we will not sit down till he comes" (1 Sam. 16:11).

And here's the scene: the seven sons of Jesse, all taller and stronger than the puny shepherd they've fetched, are standing shoulder to shoulder, and Jesse and Samuel are standing with them. Then approaches the runt named David. Little baby-faced David stands in the company of these heroic figures, looking up to them all, and God says—against all odds, in a way that turns our thinking on its head—*he's the one.*

Samuel anoints David right in front of his bigger brothers. In the shadow of their strength, surrounded by the appearances our world admires, the Spirit of God rushed upon the little guy.

Because God doesn't see as we see. That's the explanation already given to us in the story before we read about David's anointing. There is something categorically different about God when it comes to the way he looks at people. We tend to see only what we *can* see, but God sees through to the inside. God "looks on the heart," says 1 Samuel 16:7, and that opens up for us a whole new world of priority.

MEET THE HEART

The Bible has a lot to say about the heart, the Hebrew *leb* and the Greek *kardia*, as well as a few other synonyms. The concept shows up more than a thousand times throughout the Old and New Testaments, beginning as early as Genesis, and its most basic meaning lines up with the way we still use it today. The heart refers to the center of our person, the bull's-eye of who we are. It's the metaphysical organ that pumps life into everything else we think and do, which is why we call it *the heart*. As Matthew LaPine explains, "[The heart] is the holistic, inward source of agency from which *orientation flows*."[4]

> We tend to see only what we *can* see, but God sees through to the inside. God "looks on the heart."

The "heart" is perhaps the most common ancient concept in our modern language. We say it all the time, and its roots can be traced back to the foundations of mankind. People from all ages and cultures have understood the "heart" as a kind of unseen causer central to who we are. In many ways, the heart represents our truest

---

4. Matthew LaPine, "Discerning the Thoughts and Intention of the Body: Retrieving Theological Psychology," PhD diss., Trinity Evangelical Divinity School, 2018, 324.

selves. Proverbs instructs us, "As in water face reflects face, so the heart of man reflects the man" (Prov. 27:19).

This explains why we've made the heart a baseline standard for what we expect in our relational commitments, whether on the basketball court or in the bedroom. Coaches want their players to play with heart, and no spouse considers a romantic gift sincere if the heart isn't in it. That's the reason we—*and the Bible*—will say things like "in the heart" and "from the heart" and "take it to heart." When Jesus said that the Greatest Commandment is to love God *with all your heart*, we understand what he means.[5] He's talking about the realist part of the self, and he's quoting Moses, who said it centuries before him (Deut. 6:5).

Your heart is who you are, and it's the influencer of what you do, whether that influence is good or bad.

The heart has always been about wanting what it wants. It was the seventeenth-century philosopher Pascal, not a pop lyric, who said: "The heart has its reasons of which reason knows nothing." And so it's no accident that the wisest man to ever live counsels us: "Keep your heart with all vigilance, *for from it flow the springs of life*" (Prov. 4:23, emphasis added). Your heart is the source, the control panel, the joystick, from which everything else follows. Jesus taught us the same thing when he said that "out of the abundance *of the heart* the mouth speaks" (Matt. 12:34, emphasis added). This means that what we're saying and doing *out there* comes from somewhere *in here*. And the *in here* is more of who we truly are than the facades we fabricate.

---

5. See Matthew 22:37.

LED BY LOVE

Jesus was and is the foremost expert on the human heart. John tells us that Jesus didn't need anyone to explain to him how we humans work, "for he himself knew what was in man" (John 2:25). That is the kind of knowledge behind his teaching on where our words come from and where our treasure resides. As Jesus puts it, "Where your treasure is, there *your heart* will be also" (Matt. 6:21).

This brings the meaning of the heart into even more focus. Not only is the heart our truest self that influences what we do, but that influence mainly has to do with love. What we treasure is what we value and desire—*it's what we love*—and Jesus says *that* is where our heart *is*. That is what the heart is all about.

The heart is the engine of love, and because the heart is our truest self, we conclude that we are most fundamentally lovers. Thinking is important, and we should do it well, but love sits in the driver's seat of every individual.

Love sits in the driver's seat of every individual.

Most Christian thinkers throughout our history have understood love this way, going back to Augustine, stemming down through Jonathan Edwards, and agreed upon by the faithful theologians of today: "We are essentially and ultimately desiring animals, which is simply to say that we are essentially and ultimately lovers. To be human is to love, and it is what we love that defines who we are."[6] James K. A. Smith continues:

> To say that humans are, at root, lovers is to empha-
> size that we are the sorts of animals for whom
> things matter in ways that we often don't (and
> can't) articulate. There is a sort of drive (or pull,
> depending on the metaphor) that pushes (or pulls)
> us to act in certain ways, develop certain relation-
> ships, pursue certain goods, make certain sacrifices,
> enjoy certain things. And at the end of the day, if
> asked why we do this, ultimately we run up against
> the limits of articulation even though we "know"
> why we do it: it's because of what we love.[7]

This conversation can become more philosophical and dense, but a lot of times it's just plain common sense. We know that our hearts have the power. Every action we do is connected back to our hearts esteeming that action (or what it intends) as worthy—that is, as *lovable*. Ultimately, we will only do what we want to do. Therefore, when God looks on the heart, this is what he sees. He's looking through our exteriors to who we truly are, to the affections that influence us the most, and to our deepest loves. It's no wonder,

---

6. James K. A. Smith, *Desiring the Kingdom (Cultural Liturgies): Worship, Worldview, and Cultural Formation* (Grand Rapids, MI: Baker Publishing Group, 2009), Kindle locations 811–15.
7. Ibid., Kindle Locations 829–833.

then, why the heart is of most interest to God, and why it deserves our attention.

But there's a problem: the heart is also distorted.

THESE DISTORTED HEARTS

Everyone knows what we mean when we talk about broken hearts. Heartbreak is the standard euphemism for emotional pain, which is typically relational and always refers to some type of disruption. A "broken heart" is what happens when something goes wrong with the things we love, and it's unavoidable in a world full of people like us. But a distorted heart is different.

Heart distortion is a problem with the lover, not the thing loved. It is the upstream condition that contorts our ability to love rightly, and, contrary to popular opinion, the Bible says *we all have a problem here.* After sin entered the world in Genesis 3, things started to go bad quickly. The worst of it is described in Genesis 6:5: "The LORD saw that the wickedness of man was great in the earth, and that every intention of the thoughts *of his heart* was only evil continually."

In other words, human wickedness was rampant; it was so rampant, in fact, that "every intention" was "only evil continually." I don't know how the language could be more intense. The heart was *only* evil *all the time.* That's why wickedness ran wild.

Many years later, the prophet Jeremiah commented on the heart, and he wasn't any softer. Jeremiah writes, "The heart is deceitful above all things, and desperately sick; who can understand it?" (Jer. 17:9). So the heart is 1) foremost in deceit, 2) desperately sick, and 3) practically unintelligible—*that's what the Bible says about our hearts.*

And just like that, with one realistic look into the pages of Scripture, the whole pop-mantra of "follow your heart" crumbles. Who would want to follow *that*? Is *that* really the kind of driver you want behind the wheel?

GET ME OUT OF HERE

One of the worst feelings I've ever felt was in the backseat of a car. I was a freshman in high school and I was out of control, literally. It was a sunny Saturday in September during a special weekend in the town closest to where I grew up. There was an annual parade, and a rodeo, and a catalog of other festivities going on. My buddy and I were walking around downtown, bouncing from one expo to the next, trying to work our way to the end of Main Street to meet some other friends. In the midst of greeting everyone we knew, an older kid from school asked if we wanted a ride. We said yes, and climbed into his car, which made a ton of sense in the moment. We cruised over to the popular fast-food joint where our other friends were hanging out for a bite . . . except that we didn't get out of the car.

Another guy from high school pulled his car into the space beside us. He was driving another load of kids, all of them from school, and he exchanged a few words with our driver—something about whose car was faster. All of a sudden, we were peeling out of the parking lot, leaving the town limits behind.

As the roads became more rural and winding, our speed only accelerated. The other car full of kids zoomed past us, and then we zoomed past them, and it was around that time when I realized I was in the middle of an impromptu street race—and worse than the illegality of this whole ordeal, I feared for my life. I was out of control. I begged the driver to stop, to take me back to town, to get me out of here—but it didn't work. There was a maniac behind the wheel, and for all intents and purposes, he was deceptive, sick, and incoherent, *and he was taking me somewhere.* Just like our hearts.

Looking back on that car ride, there are layers of reasons why it's so memorable today, but I think the most frightening part was being forced to follow someone so completely untrustworthy. Whatever trust I had when I first climbed into that backseat evaporated as soon as we skidded out of the fast-food joint, and by that point it was too late. I wasn't very reflective as we were careening down those curvy roads, but I did wish I had already known what I was learning then. And this is where the Bible does us a favor.

Before we climb into the backseat of our hearts, we need to know something about the driver. Before we agree with the cultural clichés, or take our cues merely from what we want, we need to let Scripture pull the mask off of our inner person. It's not pretty. There's a maniac inside us, deceptive, sick, and incoherent. Watch out.

WHERE ARE YOU?

The Puritan John Owen would say the same thing. In the 1660s, Owen gave a series of lectures to college students at Oxford on the fight against sin. Those lectures still exist today in his book, *Of the Mortification of Sin in Believers.* There's only one passage from Owen I've ever memorized, and it's mainly because I can't forget it. He writes:

Be acquainted, then, with thine own heart: though
it be deep, search it; though it be dark, inquire unto
it; though it give all its distempers other names
than what are their due, believe it not.[8]

Owen doesn't hold back in his diagnosis. He says that an accurate assessment of our hearts leads to one logical conclusion: *don't trust them.* Our hearts are distorted, which means our loves are disordered. And God sees all of that.

We have these distorted hearts that drive us places we don't really want to go, and God sees, and he cares. He sees us better than anyone else, and he is concerned about our inner depths more than how we look or how others perceive us. And God is certainly not impressed by our posing. In fact, the heart farthest away from God is the heart that headlines something it's not. This is the meaning of hypocrisy, and Jesus condemned it. He said to the Pharisees:

> An accurate assessment of our hearts leads to one logical conclusion: *don't trust them.*

"You hypocrites! Well did Isaiah prophesy of you, when he said: 'This people honors me with their lips, *but their heart is far from me*; in vain do they worship me.'" (Matt. 15:7–9, emphasis added)

See, it's our hearts that matter most to God.

---

8. John Owen, *Of the Mortification of Sin in Believers* in *Overcoming Sin and Temptation: Three Classic Works by John Owen*, ed. Kelly M. Kapic and Justin Taylor (Wheaton, IL: Crossway, 2006), 203.

We can also hear this in God's first question to Adam after sin entered the world. In the wreckage of his rebellion, as the curse was already seeping into God's good design, God came to Adam and asked him a simple question: "Where are you?" (Gen. 3:9).

Where are you?

Adam and Eve were hiding, of course. God knew *that*. But his question was about something deeper, and it's a question God still asks us today. Chip Dodd says this is the question God repeatedly puts to our hearts, and until we know the answer, we don't know where we are or where we're going.[9] Until we can be honest with God about the mess inside us, we're lost. And David knew that in Psalm 51.

We don't know all the details about how David's heart degenerated from a heart after God's own to a heart after another man's wife.[10] It can be disturbing and confusing, really, for us to chase that rabbit. What exactly was happening when David sinned and then repented? Was he "regenerate" before the Bathsheba fiasco or not? Didn't the Spirit rush upon him that day in front of his brothers?

It's hard to comment with precision about the order and degree of the Spirit's work in David's life. I don't know the exact moment when David was born again—in fact, I don't even know that about myself—but what we do know about David is what he says in Psalm 51 *about his heart.*

At the very least, in Psalm 51 David knew in some deeper way what he had already known before: God doesn't give a hoot about

---

9. Chip Dodd, *The Voice of the Heart: A Call to Full Living* (Nashville, TN: Sage Hill Resources, 2014), Kindle locations 63–65.
10. See Acts 13:22.

religious appearances, but he delights in a "broken and contrite heart" (Ps. 51:17). God is attentive to our inward being, and it's from the inside-out where God wants us to learn his ways.[11]

David had finally come to grips with how badly he had veered off course. He would say later, in Psalm 101:4, "A perverse heart shall be far from me; I will know nothing of evil"—but in Psalm 51 the perverse heart was *within him*, and *he had done the evil*. And so if God had asked David what he asked Adam, "Where are you?," David would have owned it—just as he did own it when Nathan confronted him as God's spokesman.[12]

We may not experience a dramatic confrontation like David, but we all need an honest answer to what's going on inside. Suppose that God asks you, right now, "Where are you?" *Hey, child, I'm talking to you. You, reading this book. You, right now. Where are you? Where is your heart?*

If God were talking to us, would we know what to say? Sometimes seeing our hearts can be a little murkier than others, but I've found it helpful to keep routine contact. That starts in the morning by praying this prayer, by getting a moment in the quiet, before the day is upon us. Other routines that might help are developing the self-awareness to recognize our pricklier emotions before they grab the wheel. We all have our proclivities, and we should know them as well as we know the kind of swimmers we are. Not just anyone jumps into the Iron Man race, and for good reason. My wife was a lifeguard in high school, and as all lifeguards know, the

---

11. See Psalm 51:6.
12. See 2 Samuel 12:13.

most dangerous thing about the water is the poor self-assessment of the people in it.

This is also where relationships can become such a blessing. We each need people in our lives who can shoot it straight. We need people who ask us "How are you?" and really want to know. And we need to be those kinds of people for others. That simple question, "How are you?," is a simple invitation for a heart check-in. Whether we process it aloud or not, those moments, even in chit-chat, are reminders that we are something—*our hearts are somewhere*—and it matters to God. God cares and he knows.

There is no hiding in Psalm 51. Augustine says that nothing is nearer to God's ears than a confessing heart, and that's exactly what we see in David's repentance. The heart is open and exposed, and David is getting real: *My heart is who I truly am, God, and it matters most to you. My heart is so distorted, and you can see it all. God, look at me. I'm a mess.*

THE LAST-DITCH SOLUTION

We're stuck, you know—you, me, all we humans like David. We have these hearts that matter so much to God, and they're terribly distorted, and we understand the predicament. We own our problem like David did because we know it's true, but where do we go from here?

Once again we follow David's lead. The only real option for dealing with hearts like ours is to ask God for a new one. That's the prayer of Psalm 51:10, "Create in me a clean heart, O God, and renew a right spirit within me."

The first word in this petition is the verb *create*—which is also the very first verb of the entire Bible. It all started in Genesis 1:1: "In the beginning, God *created* the heavens and the earth."

David is using this same word in Psalm 51, and it has the same meaning. It refers to the divine act of making something exist that did not exist. The theological phrase for this is *creation ex nihilo*, which means "creation out of nothing." It is meant to highlight the fact that there was absolutely nothing before God spoke the world into existence. He didn't start by stumbling through a forsaken universe collecting scrap parts. He didn't collaborate with bits of matter scattered in outer space. At one time—the time before time began, the space before God spoke—there was *nothing*. There was only God in his triune fellowship as Father, Son, and Holy Spirit. It was God alone, together with himself, apart from any created thing. But then God spoke and *created* the heavens and earth, which means that now everything that exists, everything in the universe, goes back to that one decisive moment when God *acted*.

And in the same way that God created the world, David is asking God to create in him a clean heart. He needs God to bring into existence things that do not exist. He needs God to make a way where there is no way. David knows that's the kind of power it's going to take. And therefore, in a very real sense, David's prayer in Psalm 51:10 is the humblest prayer we could ever pray. It's our only chance, our last-ditch solution.

> David's prayer in Psalm 51:10 is the humblest prayer we could ever pray. It's our only chance, our last-ditch solution.

David knew—*and we know*—that once we go there, once we petition God for his creative power, we've finally resigned all hope in our own efforts. We can't ask for God to *create* and then try to meet him halfway, or any part of the way. This is not a rehabilitation project. When we've requested God's creative power, it means we've simultaneously renounced lobbing the smallest molecule into the mix. God must *create*. This is our last hope. We cannot do this; only God can—*so will you, God?*

It's not by accident that the language of Psalm 51 sends us back to the book of Genesis. David perhaps had a bookmark in Genesis 1 because he understood that a new creation would be the only way to undo his reenactment of Genesis 3. There is a curious similarity between the infamous fall of mankind in the garden of Eden[13] and David's "fall" on the rooftop of his palace.[14] It has to do with an insidious cocktail of three words that follow the tempter's confrontation of Eve: she "saw" that the tree was "good" and then she "took" its fruit. *Saw, good, took*—all in defiance of God's clear command.

And what about David on his rooftop?

He *saw* Bathsheba, considered her *beautiful* (the same Hebrew word for *good*), and then he *took* her.

David's actions feature the exact three words we see in Genesis 3—because this is the same kind of defiance. The kingly vicegerent has once again rejected the commands of God, attempting to put himself on God's throne. He has overstepped boundaries, naming desirable what God has prohibited. David has repeated mankind's fall into sin. He did what the first humans did, and what we've all

---

13. See Genesis 3:6–7.
14. See 2 Samuel 11:2–4.

done ever since—and he knew the only way out would mean God going back to the start.

FIX ME FIRST

David wasn't asking for a new world out there—at least not yet. In Psalm 51, in this earnest plea for mercy, in this last-ditch solution, David was asking for a new heart *in him*. I think that point is significant. "Create *in me* a clean heart, O God, and renew a right spirit *within me*." It might sound pretty basic, but this kind of praying is not easy.

The default mode for humans in the midst of difficult circumstances is not to accept responsibility. Think back to the garden of Eden after the fall into sin: God came to Adam first, but then Adam blamed Eve, and then Eve blamed the serpent (they were actually both blaming God).[15] But in Psalm 51 David makes an important break from his ancestors. He makes a confession, which is entirely different from blame-shifting. David is trying to call it the way God sees it. Before he gets into the details, he is asking God to fix him first, and we can learn something here.

It feels safe to say that most of the time when things don't go the way we want, we don't usually stop and ask God to work in us. We would rather God change the circumstances, right? We want the problem to go away. We would rather God change the things we're dealing with than change the person who's dealing with them (which is you or me).

---

15. See Genesis 3:12–13.

We all can be guilty of this, but even if it's not clicking yet, I'm sure you've seen this before. Everybody has that friend (maybe you are that friend?) who seems to bounce around from job to job, and every job they leave always has something wrong with it. It was the boss (again), or the coworkers (again), or the lack of fulfillment (again), and so they keep moving around and doing this thing over and over. Every place they end up has another problem, and at some point you just have to hit pause and say: *Okay, hold on a minute. Have you ever considered that maybe the problem isn't just your situation, but maybe the problem is you?*

We all need to ask ourselves that question.

Is there a problem with me?

Go ahead and ask that, and let me save you some time: the answer is *yes*.

Part of the problem is all of us. That doesn't mean we should walk around burdened with shame and guilt. It doesn't mean we own things we shouldn't own—unsubstantiated apologies are as gross as flattery. To know there's a problem in us simply means that we understand our need, and that whatever the situation might be, we are desperate for God's mercy applied to our hearts. We need God to fix us first. Before we want God to make all the corrections out there and in *them*, we need God to make all the corrections in here . . . in *me*.

So I'm going to say it, and I mean it: For most everything you encounter on an average, daily basis, your greatest need is not a change of your situation, it's a change of you. David shows us how to pray that way: *God, create in me a clean heart! Do the work in me first.*

WHEN GOD IS REAL

David knows that the condition of his heart requires a new work from God, and that it has to start with him. And then there is the audience of his prayer. This is where we land the plane.

David is praying to God and no one else. That might seem obvious to us, but David wants to make it clear. In verse 4, just a few sentences into his prayer, he says to God: "Against you, and you only, have I sinned and done what is evil in your sight . . ." (Ps. 51:4). But wait a minute—we know that's not entirely accurate, is it? He sinned against Bathsheba. He sinned against her husband, Uriah. He sinned against the entire nation of Israel by abdicating his vocation of holiness.[16] David has sinned against everybody, really, but here he looks to God, only God, and he says, "My sin is against *you.*"

And he's right.

He is not dismissing others here, and he doesn't forget the pain he's caused. The carnage of his sin would have been everywhere around him. Could he ever walk on his rooftop again? Could he ever look Nathan straight in the face? Could he ever ask for and expect the respect of his soldiers? Of the women whom he was called to serve and lead as king?

David had done a terrible thing, and he was suffering the consequences at every horizontal level imaginable, but in this prayer he bows his head and admits the real problem. *My sin is against you, God.* This is when David snapped back to reality, and it only makes sense to us if we know that God is real. God is more real, more

---

16. See Deuteronomy 17:19.

aware, and more near than anyone else, and it is sin against him
that makes us so desperate for mercy. Distorted hearts lead to disordered loves, which lead to disrupted worship. And where worship is
broken, people will be broken. As Andy Crouch explains, injustice
is the result of idolatry.[17] If we don't see and honor God for who
he is, then we won't see and honor his image-bearing creatures. So
David isn't skipping any steps here; he's just going to the heart of his
problem—which comes back to the heart within him.

It's the heart that God best sees and knows, the heart that is
most offensive, and the heart that God most cares about. That's
why it's the heart that David begs God to change. *Create in me a
clean heart, O God. You've got to create, and it has to be in me, and I'm
looking to you alone.*

I want that too, and I need that . . . every day.

•————————•

It's *me*, God. You know. I want to get in on your praise; I want to
join the chorus of your adoration; but then I have this heart. You
know my heart, God, because you see everything in it, and what I
need so badly, before I even take my next breath—*I need you to create
in me a clean heart, O God.* I need you to change me from the inside-
out, and I need you to do it again and again. You have replaced the
old stone with a heart of flesh, but it's still a mess without your
mercy. I need your new mercy for each moment . . . *for right now.*
O God, help me. I'm walking into this day full of difficulty. There
will be circumstances I don't like and problems I don't want, but the

---

17. Andy Crouch, *Playing God: Redeeming the Gift of Power* (Downers
Grove, IL: IVP Press, 2013).

biggest problem is my heart. Father, do in me what only you can do. I need you to change me. "Create in me a clean heart, O God, and renew a right spirit within me." *Father, change me from the inside-out!* In the name of Jesus, amen.

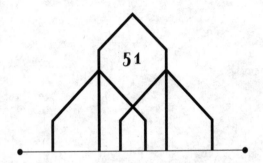

CAST ME NOT AWAY FROM YOUR PRESENCE,

AND TAKE NOT YOUR HOLY SPIRIT FROM ME.

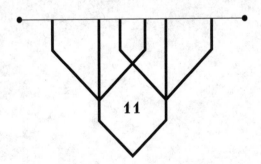

4

PRESENCE

PSALM 51:11

This might be the most earnest petition in the Bible.

Of course we don't know exactly how David looked when he made it to this moment of Psalm 51. We can't hear the tone of his voice as he prayed, and we can't see the expression on his face as he penned the words. From an exegetical perspective, there is nothing about verse 11 that makes it stand out from the petitions surrounding it—it's just another straightforward request like the others, and in one sense, aren't they all earnest?

But then, in another sense, in terms of the content here—in terms of what David is actually asking of God—Psalm 51:11 is the most earnest petition imaginable. That's because David is asking God not to leave him.

God, don't leave me.

Every Christian at some point prays something like that. Whether we say words identical to David's or whether it's a groaning deep from the heart, everybody who knows God has needed

God's nearness in the same way that David does in Psalm 51:11. And if you've been there before, you know what I mean.

As we ourselves read and pray this verse—as we pray like humans in need of mercy for today—our greatest joy and our greatest fear collide. To have God near is the wonder of heaven, but to not have God, to experience his absence, to be stranded, is *hell*. Nobody wants to be alone, and most certainly not left alone by God. That's why David prays what he does. That's why it's so earnest.

God, don't leave me. Please don't leave me!

There is a lot going on behind these words, both at the level of reality and at the level of David's experience. Both levels are worth understanding. As we have seen in the previous chapters, the world outside ourselves is the real world, but our interaction with that world matters. When it comes to God's presence, there is the truth of his presence with or without us, and then there is the difference that truth makes in our lives.

THE STORY OF PRESENCE

The presence of God is a topic that's easy to relegate to a strictly private realm. Are we talking about our own feelings here? Is this the warm and fuzzies? What does *presence* mean?

Well, in Psalm 51:11 David mentions the presence of God in connection to the Holy Spirit, who is neither theoretical nor emotional, but personal. David understands that with God "your presence" is the same as "your Holy Spirit." And so by citing God's presence and the third person of the Holy Trinity, David is tapping into one of the greatest themes in the entire Bible.

The theme starts in Genesis and runs all the way through the end of Revelation. While it would be far beyond the scope of this little book to mention every instance of the Spirit's activity, I do want to highlight four mile-markers throughout Scripture where we see the theme of his activity develop. It goes like this:

1. Presence Lost
2. Presence Promised
3. Presence Realized
4. Presence Secured

1. Presence Lost

The story of God's presence starts back in Genesis when he created Adam and Eve. The Bible tells us that God created Adam, and all mankind, in his image and likeness. Humanity's purpose was to resemble and reflect God and to do that in the presence of God. That was the reality in the garden of Eden. God placed Adam in the garden and commanded him to "work it and keep it" *in fellowship with God.*[1]

But in Genesis 3 Satan tempted Adam and Eve, and they fell into sin. Then came the curse. Everything was tainted, for the man, for the woman, for all creation around them. And yet the worst part of the curse was actually the last thing mentioned in Genesis 3. It was that Adam and Eve were exiled from the garden. They were practically castaways. God "drove them out" of Eden, which means that the presence of God Adam and Eve first enjoyed was now *lost*. The people of God were separated from the presence of God. Sin

---

1. See Genesis 2:15; 3:8.

brought the separation, and therefore, humanity could no longer come near to God. They didn't have the same kind of fellowship. That's Presence Lost.

2. Presence Promised

The story, of course, doesn't end there. Because God is merciful, he was determined to save his people. God resolved to reconcile the relationship between himself and humanity, so he put into motion his plan for redemption.

We see this plan first in God's promise to Adam and Eve that the woman's offspring would crush the head of the serpent.[2] Then we see it with Noah and the ark—the world was wicked, and God brought judgment on everything, but he saved Noah and his family because God had grace on him.[3] And then we see it in God's call of Abraham whose whole life is a showcase of grace. God came to Abraham *because God wanted to*—simple as that—and God made him a promise that through his offspring all the nations of the earth would be blessed.

> The people of God were separated from the presence of God. Sin brought the separation, and therefore, humanity could no longer come near to God.

That promise also included land. God promised Abraham, and later his descendants, the people of Israel, that he would give them *a place.* It was called the land of Canaan, or the Promised Land, and

2. See Genesis 3:15.
3. See Genesis 6:8.

the first five books of the Bible are mainly about how God brings his people to that land, from slavery in Egypt and then through wandering in the desert for forty years. It's amazing how the Bible describes God's presence with his people during their sojourning. God went before them "by day in a pillar of a cloud to lead them along the way, and by night in a pillar of fire to give them light" (Exod. 13:21–22). That was God's presence with them.

After they crossed the Red Sea, they came to Mount Sinai, and God's presence dwelled on the top of the mountain as a consuming fire.[4] And then in Exodus 25, God instructed the people of Israel to build him a sanctuary called the tabernacle; this was the place where God said he would dwell in their midst.[5] That's a big deal in light of human history up to this point.

In the tabernacle was the ark of the covenant, and there in the ark, at what was called the mercy seat, God said he would "meet" with his people through the priesthood.[6] *Dwelling. Meeting!* This was glorious. God was with his people! But still, they weren't at the place God promised them, and they still didn't enjoy God's presence like Adam first did in the garden.

So a little later, through the conquests led by Joshua, and despite the roller-coaster period led by the judges, the people of God eventually landed in the Promised Land. Against all odds, they made it.

Then came the kings, the greatest of which was David, who wrote Psalm 51. David was determined to build a house for God in

---

4. See Exodus 16:18.
5. See Exodus 25:8.
6. See Exodus 25:22.

Jerusalem, a place for God to permanently dwell with his people. He thought God deserved a real house—not a make-shift tent like the tabernacle. The house would be called the temple, and the temple of God would become another way to talk about the presence of God himself.

But God didn't let David build it. Instead, David's son Solomon built the temple, and the Bible tells us it was a beautiful structure full of splendor. The inside of the temple, in the inner sanctuary, actually resembled a garden. It was made of cedar and olivewood, and it had carvings of palm trees and flowers.[7] And best of all, in the temple was the Most Holy Place, where the ark of the covenant stayed. There, in the ark, God's presence filled the temple like a cloud.[8]

All of this was wonderful. It was like the tabernacle, but better—and yet, still, it wasn't the same as the garden . . . and it wasn't permanent.

And after a string of bad kings and the people's idolatry, God's presence left the temple, and foreign powers came in and destroyed Jerusalem. In the same way that Adam and Eve were exiled from the garden because of sin, the people of Israel were exiled from Jerusalem because of sin. Once again there was separation between God and his people—and the people of God languished in this separation.

So then came the prophets. Men of God came to God's people as his spokesman, and they told about a day in the future when God would once again dwell with his people. The prophet Isaiah talked

7. See 1 Kings 6:32.
8. See 1 Kings 8:6, 10–11.

about how one day there would be this son who would be born, whose name would be called Immanuel, which means God with us.[9] Jeremiah talked about how God was going to bring Israel back to the place of his presence, that he would be their God.[10] Ezekiel came and said that God would actually put his Spirit *within* his people, would actually dwell among them *forever*, and would take their land that had become desolate because of sin and make it like the Garden of Eden.[11]

Isaiah knew all about that, too. He said this new land would actually be a new heaven and a new earth, and would be a place unlike anything we could ever imagine. It would be even *better* than the garden.[12] In fact, it seems almost crazy how Isaiah talks about this place—

- as a place of only joy and gladness: "no more shall be heard in it the sound of weeping" or the cry of distress.[13]
- as a place of unparalleled peace: the wolf and lamb will graze together, and the lion is going to eat straw like an ox.[14]
- as a place of universal praise: all flesh will come and worship God.[15]

9. See Isaiah 7:14.
10. See Jeremiah 32:36–41.
11. See Ezekiel 37:14; 36:35.
12. See Isaiah 66:22–23.
13. See Isaiah 65:19.
14. See Isaiah 65:25.
15. See Isaiah 66:23.

Most amazing of all, though, is that this new heaven and new earth will be the place where God *forever dwells with his people*. That was the promise.

That's the Presence Promised, and it's basically the whole Old Testament.

3. Presence Realized

In the New Testament, we see the Presence Realized. In the Gospel of Matthew, we read about Jesus, who is called Immanuel, God with us—just like Isaiah had said.

Jesus is the promised Son, the anticipated Messiah who is not just the Savior for Israel, but for all of humanity. No longer was the presence of God a fire on top of a mountain or a cloud contained to an inner sanctuary, but now the presence of God became a person like us.

Jesus *is* God with us, who walked among us and lived life in our shoes and dwelled in our details. *Jesus was God's presence realized*— and he looked people like us in the face. People touched him and talked to him and heard from him. Think about that. What does it mean to see a person in real life? To hear their voice? To somehow touch their flesh with your hands, with a handshake, a hug, a pat on the back? Real people like you and me had contact with Jesus, and Jesus was straightforward about what he was doing. He said that *to see him was to have seen God the Father*.[16]

Then on the night before Jesus was crucified, he was having dinner with his disciples, and he began to tell them about the

---

16. See John 14:9.

Helper, his Spirit, whom he was going to send to be with them forever. After his death in our place, and after his resurrection from the dead, and after his ascension back to the Father, Jesus said he was going to send his Spirit to live in his people as *his actual presence with them.*

The Holy Spirit had been active in the world since the beginning,[17] and he was at work in the people of God throughout their history—David talks about him in Psalm 51. But what Jesus promised us about the Spirit was going to be new and different. This time, the Holy Spirit was going to be poured out on all of God's people, which means that better than a fire on top of a mountain and a cloud in the inner sanctuary, now the presence of God will dwell inside God's people by his Spirit.

Jesus said that when the Holy Spirit comes, God is going to make his home in everyone who trusts him.[18] Presence Realized is what brings us to the Presence Secured.

4. Presence Secured

The apostle Paul is the most prominent theologian of the Holy Spirit there has ever been. He shows us, over and over again, how the Holy Spirit in us changes everything. The Holy Spirit is one who gives us both character and confidence (Rom. 5:4–5).

- He's the love of God poured into our hearts (Rom. 5:5).

---

17. See Genesis 1:2.
18. See John 14:23.

- He's the life of God for victory over sin (Rom. 8:11).
- He's the proof of God that we're his children (Rom. 8:16).
- He's the knowledge of God who gives us wisdom (1 Cor. 2:12).
- He's the power of God for our obedience (Gal. 5:25).
- He's the fuel of God for our faith (1 Cor. 12:3).
- He's the peace of God who unites us together (Eph. 4:5–6).
- He's the gift of God for all our ministry (1 Cor. 12:7).
- He's the minster of God for all our gifts (1 Cor. 12:11).
- He's the boldness of God when we're afraid (2 Tim. 1:7).
- He's the comfort of God in our sorrow (Rom. 8:26).
- He's the joy of God in our affliction (1 Thess. 1:6).
- He's the worker of God in our worship (Phil. 3:3).
- He's the seal of God who will keep us forever (2 Cor. 1:22).
- He's the guarantee of God for a glorious future (Eph. 1:13–14).

And we could keep going, because the Bible keeps going. Can we truly fathom the wonder of the Holy Spirit? Of *God* dwelling in *us*? It is happily bewildering.

I'm not from a charismatic background where spontaneous laughter erupts in worship—it would be strange if our church did that—but laughter seems about right when we grasp the meaning and power of the Spirit. What emotions should we have? We laugh sometimes because we're filled with joy, and sometimes because we're nervous—maybe recognizing that the Spirit of God dwells in us produces joy *and* a little nervousness! And seriously, I can't help but laugh as I write this—it is just too wondrous.

And of all the promises of the Spirit, there is one that encompasses the rest. Paul says that because the Holy Spirit dwells within us, we are now the temple of God. "Do you not know that you are God's temple and that God's Spirit dwells in you?" (1 Cor. 3:16).

We as God's people, because God's Spirit is within us, *are God's dwelling place.*

FROM HERE TO FOREVER

The implications of this truth are staggering, and it's something that I've had to embrace personally. Through July 2017 our church plant had been meeting at a school in south Minneapolis for two and a half years. It was a very nice building for a scrappy church plant. The chapel was spacious and the chairs were the soft, folding kind that are bolted to the floor. We had grown into the place and our numbers were multiplying, but then, on Wednesday morning, August 2, 2017, there was an accidental gas explosion that decimated the property. Two individuals lost their lives in the explosion, and the school was forced to move. As I am writing this, the rebuilding project for that property is still underway.

Needless to say, our church had to figure out where to meet for worship. That meant a theater one Sunday, and then a couple of different college campuses for several months until we found a longer term leasing option. The nomadism that overtook us wasn't exactly recommended in the conventional church planting manuals. We had always said that "the church is the people, not the building"—but we found ourselves in a place (or lack of place) where we had to believe it was true.

So we told our church each Sunday, wherever we were meeting, that God is dwelling in the spaces we inhabit because God's Spirit is dwelling in us. God's presence isn't a holy place where his people must go; his presence is in his holy people who go everywhere. And in fact, *in our going*, Jesus promises to never leave us: "Behold, I am with you always, to the end of the age" (Matt. 28:20). The Holy Spirit says that no matter where we go, no matter where we end up, even if it's up in highest heavens or down to the uttermost parts of the sea, God will be with us.[19]

> The Holy Spirit says that no matter where we go, no matter where we end up, even if it's up in highest heavens or down to the uttermost parts of the sea, God will be with us.

God will be with his people, and that's what heaven will be.

In the book of Revelation, the last book of the Bible, John envisions what Isaiah had foretold so many years before.

19. See Psalm 139:8–10.

Behold, the dwelling place of God is with man. He
will dwell with them, and they will be his people,
and God himself will be with them as their God.
(Rev. 21:3)

The presence of God is our purpose—lost, promised, realized,
and secured. Everything in this world is trending toward Revelation
21:3. This is what God intended back in the garden, and it's what
God accomplishes through the gospel of his Son.

When we see David mention God's presence in Psalm 51, we
should know the meaning of God's presence in the Bible. David
isn't simply concerned about losing a feeling. It's not about the
warm fuzzies. David is pleading with God: *Do not remove your presence from me. Do not leave me. Do not take your Spirit from me.*

It's an urgent plea, and there's more.

GOD'S NEARNESS IS OUR GOOD

There is the truth about God's presence, which the Bible gives
us, but then there is also the human experience of God's presence,
which we find in the psalms. More than a fact that we acknowledge,
God's presence is a reality we ought to *desire*. It is something we
value, something we want. The nearness of God is our joy.

That's the way it's put in Psalm 73:25. After the psalmist has
contemplated his own sin (vv. 1–3) and the absurd flourishing of
the wicked (vv. 4–17), he comes back to God by seeing the larger
picture. God is with him, and God is enough. Indeed—

> Who do I have in heaven but you? And I desire
> nothing on earth but you. My flesh and my heart
> may fail, but God is the strength of my heart, my
> portion forever. Those far from you will certainly
> perish; you destroy all who are unfaithful to you.
> But as for me, God's presence is my good. I have
> made the Lord GOD my refuge, so I can tell about
> all you do. (Ps. 73:25–28 CSB)

For the psalmist, the presence of God is more than a biblical theme—*the presence of God is his good.*

David shows us the same thing in Psalm 143. He begins that psalm in darkness, having been pursued and crushed by his enemies.[20] He is appalled, undone, desperate for God's help, and so he prays:

> Answer me quickly, O LORD!
> My spirit fails!
> Hide not your face from me,
> lest I be like those who go down to the pit. (Ps. 143:7)

"Hide not your face from me." *God, don't leave me*—that's what David is asking, and he knows that's what makes all the difference. God's presence is what separates him from those who go down to the pit, from those who grovel in shame and defeat. God's presence is the game-changer. And didn't Moses say the same thing?

---

20. See Psalm 143:3.

Much earlier in Israel's history, Moses was God's chosen leader to rescue the people from Egypt and bring them to the Promised Land.[21] That was Moses's mission, but he knew he couldn't do it alone.

> And [God] said, "My presence will go with you,
> and I will give you rest." And [Moses] said to him,
> "If your presence will not go with me, do not bring
> us up from here. For how shall it be known that I
> have found favor in your sight, I and your people?
> Is it not in your going with us, so that we are dis-
> tinct, I and your people, from every other people
> on the face of the earth?" (Exod. 33:14–16)

God, I can't go if you won't go with me. Your presence is my only hope. Your nearness is my good. Moses says it. The psalmists say it. And David says it.

That is also what we must say if we are going to pray Psalm 51:11 after David. When David pleaded, "Cast me not away from your presence," he understood, like so many others in the Bible, that the presence of God is more than a theological category. David had known what it meant to be near God, and he knew he didn't want to be far from God. *Don't bar me from your fellowship, please. I can't do this without you.* "Cast me not away from your presence and take not your Holy Spirit from me." *God, please don't leave me.*

---

21. See Exodus 33:1–3.

MORE THAN ANSWERS

David's prayer is so earnest, as Calvin puts it, because he is asking to "not be deprived of what he had justly forfeited." In other words, David knew he had messed up and that he did not deserve the presence of God. He did not deserve the nearness of God, but he needed it so badly, and that's why he pleaded for it.

Truth is, every Christian at some point is going to be where David found himself. It may not be because you've done what David did, but eventually you will understand that you have the same need for God. Your need is great and you're entitled to nothing. That's the place I'm talking about. And whenever you find yourself there, however you get there, there is one thing I hope you remember. Really, in God's kindness, I pray that you remember: *We need God's Spirit more than we need his answers.*

Often when hardship comes, we tend to get right into the questions. We want to know *why.* We want to discern God's design on the other side of these details: *maybe God is doing this? Or this? Or this?* We want answers, and that's okay. There is such a thing as a holy humility that presses in with God and says, "Father, what are you doing?" The psalms do that, and we can do that in faith.

We need God's Spirit more than we need his answers.

But even in our asking *why*—as we are seeking answers from God—eventually we will come to a place where we mainly just need his nearness. And in that place of hardship and suffering, our most earnest prayer will not be for an explanation of our circumstances, but for God not to leave us. That's because we know that wherever he brings us, however this situation plays out, as long as he is with us, ultimately everything will be all right—and I mean that in the deepest sense of "all" and the deepest sense of "right."

God is creating a new heavens and a new earth. Revelation 21:3 is our destiny. His nearness is our good.

God, open my lips and my mouth will declare your praise. You are worthy of all praise, and indeed, you will be praised. *Let me get in on it!* And God, I need you to change my heart, which means I need you to create in me a new one. I need you to do with my heart what only you can do. *Change me from the inside out!* And God, whatever comes, wherever I find myself at the end of this day, I need your presence. I don't know exactly where you're leading me, but I know I can't do it without your Spirit. I just can't. And I don't want to. God, be close to me, please. Be near. "Cast me not away from your presence and take not your Holy Spirit from me." *God, please don't leave me.*

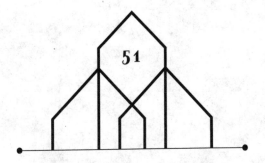

RESTORE TO ME THE JOY OF YOUR SALVATION,

AND UPHOLD ME WITH A WILLING SPIRIT.

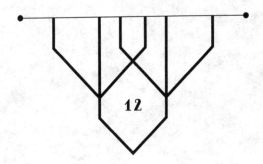

5

JOY

PSALM 51:12

David is asking God for an experience. He is. There's no way around it.

In Psalm 51:12, the final petition of our four-fold prayer, David is asking God to make him know the joy of God's salvation, which means, David's not *just* asking for an experience, but he's asking for an experience of an *emotion*.

Could there be any two words combined that are more sketchy for "Bible-centered Christians" like myself? Don't we inherently distrust emotional experiences, saying that our faith needs to rest on facts, not on feelings? It seems so slippery and subjective, so personal and mysterious. David wants to feel a particular sentiment. He wants firsthand knowledge of joy. It's right there in the Bible, in Psalm 51:12, "Restore to me the joy of your salvation . . ." *God, give me joy again!*

EXPERIENCE AGAIN

We've talked a lot about experience in this book because we've been talking about prayer, and prayer is the bridge-builder between truth and experience. Prayer is when we wrestle the unchanging truths of God into personal relevance. At the same time, I've cautioned against undermining the moral framework of God's world. God is God outside of us, and that means our experience of God determines nothing about the truth of God.

As with most of reality, we're compelled to avoid two extremes. One extreme says experience is in control. It's the experiential-expressive approach to religion, as it's been called. This is where truth claims are ignored and faith is reduced to practice—"my religion *is* my experience." That won't fly.

The other extreme is to smother experience and reduce Christian faithfulness to simply approving true propositions about God. This is where correct doctrine is equated with spiritual maturity—"my religion *is* my theology." But that's not right either.

An underlying conviction in this book is something like an integrated approach: a third way embraces God outside of us and also values our experience of him.

I believe this "third way" is the historic Christian approach to spirituality, and the big reason it's worth emphasizing today is because of our cultural moment. The idea of religion as solely experience is hot, and the push for tolerance (even hotter) depends upon it. So much is riding on this. Think about it: if religious commitment is only experience, then who are we to make any valuations of one commitment over another? Whose personal experience gets the gold medal? The answer is none. Because experience flies under the radar of any objective barometer. This leads to a kind of mis-guided pluralism where coexistence requires equal validation. D. A. Carson has called this the "new tolerance," and it's still going strong as the leading ideology in America. To disapprove of this ideology is often considered bigotry.[1]

So for the past couple of centuries, and maybe more than ever today, Christians at large have become pretty self-conscious. We really don't want to be called bigots—it's like the evangelical kryp-tonite. So we've had to carefully review the road that led us to where we are, watching our steps like we're learning a new line-dance. And while that's okay at one level—it's good to be watchful—even-tually we have to stop looking at our feet. Christian faithfulness doesn't just two-step, after all; it has a direction, a goal. And what if I told you that the goal is what David is asking for in this final petition? What if I told you the goal is *joy*?

THE LONGING FOR REAL JOY

We all want what David wants in Psalm 51:12 because every human wants to be happy. *Give me joy, God, because my heart is starv-ing for joy.* That's true of David, and it's true of you and me. But what *kind* of joy?

David, speaking to God, calls it "the joy of your salvation."

That tells us that this joy is more than a mere emotion, but still not less. We should be careful not to overdo the meaning. When David says "joy," he basically means what you would imagine he

---

1. D. A. Carson, *The Intolerance of Tolerance* (Grand Rapids, MI: Eerdmans, 2012).

means. He's talking about real joy—happiness, gladness, cheerfulness, mirth.

There is probably an image that comes into your mind when you think about those words. You might imagine someone smiling and laughing in the company of loved ones. You might remember a high point in your own life that sparked those feelings—a wedding, a party, a big game. When was the last time you couldn't help but smile?

I'm thinking, in this moment, about a text message I received a few hours ago from a good friend. It was a drop in the bucket of my entire day, but it was pleasant and humorous, and I involuntarily grinned as I read it. Life is full of that stuff, even in the dark times. We have a remarkable capacity to feel the emotion of joy and to long for it, and that is what David is talking about in Psalm 51, right in the middle of his own dark time.

Just a few verses before verse 12, David prays, "Let me hear joy and gladness; let the bones that you have broken rejoice" (Ps. 51:8). He uses the same word for "joy" in both verses 8 and 12, and that tells us that the kind of joy David is thinking about is a joy that can be *heard*. "Let me *hear* joy and gladness" means that David wants joy real enough to be expressed.

The second clause in verse 12 is also important. David prays, "Restore to me the joy of your salvation, *and uphold me with a willing spirit*" (emphasis added). Nearly every modern translation understands the "spirit" in verse 12 as referring to our spirit (not the Holy Spirit). That means the adjective "willing" is telling. The word could also be translated as eager, bountiful, or cheerful—and that's the kind of spirit David is asking to characterize him. *Sustain in me a cheerful soul,* in other words. He wants willingness and cheerfulness to mark his life.

When it's taken altogether, we get the point that David, again, means real joy, not just joy on paper. He means lived joy. He's talking about a kind of joy that you can identify, that you can imagine. He means the kind of joy you'd expect from a five-year-old on Christmas morning, or when your team wins the World Series in Game 7, or when you get a romantic night away with your spouse to celebrate your anniversary. Real, palpable joy that can be experienced—that's what David wants.

JOY IN GOD'S SALVATION

Then David gets even more specific. It's not just real joy, but it's real joy in relation to God's salvation. "Restore to me the joy *of your salvation.*" It becomes clear that David is talking about spiritual salvation in this prayer. God has indeed rescued David from the hand of his physical enemies—and we have those psalms—but in this instance, David is talking about God rescuing him from himself.

Often in the psalms, when God and salvation are mentioned together, the psalmist is talking about his own experience of salvation that God has given him. For example, we'll read, "The LORD is my light and *my salvation*" (Ps. 27:1, emphasis added), or "O LORD, my Lord, the strength of *my salvation*" (Ps. 140:7, emphasis added). The reference is to the salvation that he, the psalmist, has received *from* God. But then there are a few places where salvation is mentioned as the salvation *of* God, such as:

- Psalm 18:35—"You have given me the shield of *your salvation*."
- Psalm 69:13—"At an acceptable time, O God, in the abundance of your steadfast love answer me in *your salvation*."
- Psalm 85:7—"Show us your steadfast love, O LORD, and grant us *your salvation*."

We can begin to see that God's salvation is connected to God's love. This rings true in Psalm 51. The salvation *of* God—the salvation pertaining to God—is not a one-time event of dramatic deliverance, but rather, it is something at the heart of God's character. God's salvation refers to what is *in God* that caused David not to be hopeless even though he had every reason to lose hope. David is talking about what moves God at the most foundational level to work for our redemption. He's getting at *why* God shows mercy. It is because God *is* merciful. Mercy is not just a thing God does, but it's who God is. He is the God of tender mercy, or as the psalmists love to say, the God of "steadfast love." It's actually how David begins Psalm 51:

> Have mercy on me, O God,
> according to your steadfast love;
> according to your abundant mercy
> blot out my transgressions. (v. 1)

Show me mercy *because you are merciful*—because, as John tells us in the New Testament, "God is love" (1 John 4:8). And God's love toward us *is* his salvation. We might be afraid that we can't trust God's love because we know we aren't really that lovable, but that's exactly the point. It's a love that we can trust *precisely because* it's bound up in God's character, not our lovability. The seventeenth-century theologian John Owen captures this beautifully,

> On whom God fixes his love, it is immutable; it
> does not grow to eternity; it is not diminished at
> any time. It is an eternal love that had no begin-
> ning; that shall have no ending; that cannot be
> heightened by any act of ours, and that cannot be
> lessened by anything in us.[2]

My wife and I named our second son John Owen because of quotes like that. God's love for us is utterly free. It never changes, neither increasing nor decreasing. God's love is inexhaustible and irrevocable, which is why heaven must last forever.

Honestly, if we could only grasp God's love, if we could only understand its depths, that would be all we need to experience joy. I think that's why David is asking for the "joy *of God's salvation*." He knows he needs an unshakable foundation. David wants legitimate, lived-out joy that is produced by God himself. *He wants the real joy that comes from the love of God.*

And that's because he had experienced it before, but now it was gone.

---

2. John Owen, *Communion with God* (Edinburgh, Scotland: Banner of Truth, 1991), 120.

STARTING WITH "RESTORE"

David begins verse 12 by praying, *"Restore* to me the joy of your salvation . . ." (emphasis added). In other words, this joy is something he had experienced but lost, and now he longed to experience it again. That fact is vital for understanding this prayer and how it relates to us. The loss of joy is behind what David is asking, and haven't we all been there before?

We know what it's like when our joy diminishes. Whether it's related to something we've done or left undone, or whether it feels completely out of the blue, we know what it's like when our affections for God grow cold, or numb, or dull. We know what it's like to miss the joy of God's salvation. And maybe the most frustrating part of all is that we know, at least in our heads, that there is enough about God's salvation—*enough in his love*—that we should be endlessly happy! It's not just that God commands our joy; it's that *he has provided us the unshakable foundation to have that joy,* like the previous quote from John Owen tells us. I can tend to remember truths like that and hear from my inner football coach: *Remember God's love, man—and stop it! Stop the lack of joy. Be happy, doggone it!*

And then starts the "If only's . . ."—*If only I truly saw him! If only I really understood!* This makes sense, and it's right to think this way, but before long I'm not thinking about God anymore at all, but just about how pitiful I am in grasping him. Then comes some form of shame, or at least a malaise of *stuckness.* Sometimes it seems like we just can't get past the *blah.* We drift and spiral and can't seem to find our grip. You know what I mean. I'm talking about spiritual fog.

We've all been at that place before, and whenever we find ourselves there—maybe you're there right now—we can learn from

David. He is taking two actions with that little verb "restore." He is admitting the loss of joy, and he's fighting to get it back.

ADMITTING THE LOSS

It's not easy to admit we've lost our joy in God. I remember toward the end of college when I steered clear of one title at the campus bookstore. I was happily engaged to my wife, and we were preparing for the next chapter of our lives. My theology and entire concept of Christian ministry had undergone some seismic shifts in the previous years. I had a passionate vision and clarity about the things that mattered most, and that's why I couldn't bring myself to actually purchase the book *When I Don't Desire God*. I had been the guy who used his spare money to buy copies of *Desiring God* for his friends—and not in a pushy way, just giddy. I had applied for seminary in Minneapolis and dreamt of working for http://desiring God.org. Could I really carry around a book that openly stated I *didn't* desire God? At least I didn't think so. But then, what about it being true?

Eventually, I bought the book and devoured it. All these years later I can still remember exact places where I sat as I turned its pages. Joy in God had felt elusive to me. The ebb and flow—and too often the ebb—had finally forced me to acknowledge my discontentment. I wanted more of what I lacked.

It would have been much easier, though, to have just redefined joy. The simplest thing to do when joy feels opaque is to give joy a broad enough meaning to account for the opaqueness. Had David done that, he would have never felt a loss of joy, and then, of course, he would have never asked God to restore it. But he wanted *real joy*, remember, and so redefining joy was not an option.

The same goes for us. Before we can truly pray this prayer after David, we have to recognize that we are not as glad in God as we should be, or maybe as we used to be.

And this loss of joy might be because of blatant sin (like it was in David's case), or it might be because of intense suffering, or it might be because of physical illness, or it might be because of Satan's attacks, or it might be because technology leaves us with unexpected side-effects—we have this information glut where the news is always hot-n-ready, in our faces, at our fingertips, on our wrists. It's not that we've amused ourselves to death; it's that we've shriveled up our imaginations by replacing the weighty with the ephemeral, or whatever it is that gets to us the fastest. There's enough smog in this sin-soaked world to choke out our joy at any moment. The rush of words and images, and voices and videos, and sights and sounds, has waterboarded the breath of our souls so that we have no clue what it means to "be still, and know that [he] is God" (Ps. 46:10). Prayer is hard because email feels more practical. Facebook is more exciting. YouTube cures our boredom. And so we don't know which came first—the loss of joy in God that made us run to these distractions, or all these distractions that made us lose our joy in God.

It's both.

And we've gotten so used to making these mud pies in the slums, to jumping in the splash pads, that we're oblivious to the ocean offered to us—that is, until we slow down and read words like Psalm 51:12.

And we don't just read them, but we hear them. David is not just praying; he's wailing: "God, restore to me the joy of your salvation." *Oh, me too,* we think.

God, whatever it is that's caused this, I acknowledge that I don't love you like I want to. I don't have the joy in you that I should. Will you bring it back?

FIGHTING FOR JOY

David admitted his loss of joy, but he didn't stay there. *Restore the joy,* he cried. It means he's fighting. David is fighting for joy, and so are we when we pray this prayer after him. And when it comes to the fight for joy, we're in good company.

Long before all the distractions we have today, John Owen, once again, spoke with stunning relevance. Owen explained that God's love for us is like *himself*—it's unchanging and constant. But our love for God, on the other hand, is like *ourselves*—increasing and waning. Owen said God's love is like the sun because it's always the same in its light. But our love is like the moon because it's always getting bigger and then smaller, going back and forth between fullness and fractions, and then sometimes there are clouds.

But even though God's love is constant, unchanging, unwavering, he allows our felt experience of his love—our joy—to come and go. Sometimes God makes his love so manifest to us that it's like sunshine beaming down on our heads; but other times it's like he hides his face. Owen writes,

> Our Father will not always *chastise*, lest we be cast down; he does not always *smile*, lest we be full and

neglect him; but yet, still his love in itself is the same. When for a little moment he hides his face, yet he gathers us with everlasting kindness.[3]

And we should pray to taste that kindness. This is how we fight for the joy we miss. We ask God to make us feel his smile—knowing that even when we don't, the very asking for joy is the seed of joy that will bloom again.

That is because the experiences of desire and delight are deeply intertwined. In *When I Don't Desire God*, John Piper explains that *delight* is what we enjoy in the present and that *desire* is what we experience when the thing we enjoy is not present but coming to us in the future. In other words, delight is real-time and desire is anticipatory. And while that's true, Piper goes on to show that it's not so simple. The two experiences are more inseparable. He writes, "[D]esire is a form of the very pleasure that is anticipated with the arrival of the thing desired. It is, you might say, the pleasure itself experienced in the form of anticipation."[4] The anticipation—the experience of absence and longing and hope—is part of the joy.

And we all have experienced this in some way. It's why Friday night is often the best part of the weekend, especially for those who "live for the weekend." Friday night is still loaded with the anticipation of two more days off. The same goes for vacations. One of my favorite parts of vacation is the planning—getting my inbox to zero and setting my auto-reply and packing our suitcases for a week of

---

3. Owen, *Communion with God*, 121.
4. John Piper, *When I Don't Desire God: How to Fight for Joy*, Tenth-Anniversary Edition (Wheaton, IL: Crossway, 2013), 26.

leisure. Those are all desire-rich steps as I look ahead to delight, but the steps themselves tap into that delight.

When it comes to joy in God, the longing and anticipation for that joy counts for something too. However faint it might feel, your sense of absence and desire is a work of God in your soul, and he will fulfill it—partially in this life, at best, but completely in the new creation. In fact, the assurance of that fulfillment is the ministry of the Holy Spirit who indwells us. The Holy Spirit is why our hope for joy will not put us to shame.[5] The Holy Spirit is actually our down payment of the joy, as Paul says.[6] And in the meantime, in our desiring, the Holy Spirit is interceding for us according to the will of God.[7]

We often mistake our experience of joy for the gauge that assures us of our salvation. When we do this, our lack of joy will likely send us into a tailspin of doubts. We can wonder how anyone loved by God could feel so empty. Valleys like this are callings for us to lean into the Spirit's work. As complex as the emotional terrain might be, our salvation isn't validated by our ability to feel joy, but by the Spirit who keeps us—and who is able to keep us through the driest of deserts.

RIVERS IN THE DESERT

Negeb is a word used throughout the Old Testament, its root meaning to be dry or parched. It's the name given to the southern

---

5. See Romans 5:5.
6. See Ephesians 1:14; 2 Corinthians 1:22; 5:5.
7. See Romans 8:23–27.

part of Israel where it's all desert. The land in this region can become the kind of dry you might imagine when you see bleached yellow, cracking dirt. It used to be the kind of place where you wouldn't want to be stranded, especially in long seasons of drought. But in Psalm 126, the psalmist prays:

> Restore our fortunes, O LORD,
> like streams in the Negeb! (v. 4)

This is a daring petition. "Streams in the Negeb" means flowing water in the desert. The psalmist is asking:

> *God, restore us in a way that makes the desert turn green and brown and blue. Restore us in a way that makes the dry ground lush with life and flowing with water. God, restore us by a downpour of rain that saturates this hard soil and causes things to grow.*

The prayer is for God to make rivers in the desert.

And the psalmist knows God could do that in an instant. God could speak and the sky could gush with rain. God could say the word and the sulkiest soul could sing with all its might. But notice how the psalmist continues in verses 5–6:

> Those who sow in tears
> shall reap with shouts of joy!
> He who goes out weeping,
> bearing the seed for sowing,
> shall come home with shouts of joy,
> bringing his sheaves with him.

The longing for streams in the desert turns into the grueling process of sowing with tears. The image is a farmer in his toil, stepping and sowing, stepping and sowing, weeping all over the dry ground—wondering if it's ever going to end, if he's ever going to see the harvest. And the psalmist, like the farmer, honestly doesn't know. He doesn't know if all the sowing will work, except for the promise of God: "Those who sow in tears shall reap with shouts of joy!"

The joy will come—yes it will! The joy we miss, that somehow we lost, is joy we will feel again. So keep sowing. Keep longing. Keep desiring and asking and waiting for it. *That* is the fight, even as our energy wanes and we feel like giving up. The Spirit won't let us—and *he* is our assurance.

"Weeping may tarry for the night, but joy comes with the morning" (Ps. 30:5). "Why are you cast down, O my soul, and why are you in turmoil within me? Hope in God; for I shall again praise him, my salvation and my God" (Ps. 43:5). Or, as William Cowper put it:

> Judge not the Lord by feeble sense
> But trust Him for His grace
> Behind a frowning providence
> He hides a smiling face.[8]

---

8. William Cowper, "God Moves in a Mysterious Way" (1774).

And *one day we will see his smiling face.* We will absolutely see it, and until then, we fight by groaning with hope.[9] God will restore our joy. On purpose.

JOY ON PURPOSE

My family and I love calling Minnesota home—most of the time (just barely most of the time). For several months of the year, there's this thing called Winter, and it's brutal. The feeling of sub-zero wind gusts is humbling, to say the least, and it's part of the reason I became intrigued by the Dutch athlete Wim Hof.

Wim Hof is considered an extreme athlete because he has learned to mentally control his body temperature. The spectacle of this ability is that he can stand outside in his underwear in the middle of deadly cold conditions. Just Google him. Basically, he can sit in the snow unscathed when it's 30 degrees below zero.

The more you read about Wim Hof, the more you'll hear about the Eastern breathing techniques and meditation he uses. He has led seminars and tutorials about it, even published a couple of books, all so that you too can learn how to sit naked in the snow. It is intriguing, no doubt, but it raises the question: "Why?"

Well, true of Eastern meditation in general, the quest for enlightenment is a quest for experience, which is epitomized in nirvana, the ultimate peace of mind and liberation from the world. Put simply, the whole thing terminates on *me* being emptied of *me*. But here's the kicker: less of me for the sake of me is still . . . all about me. *Now how is joy in God different?* Other than the gospel intending

---

9. See Romans 8:23.

our ultimate fullness, the exact opposite of Eastern religions, how does the gospel answer the question of "Why?"

Among countless differences, one fundamental difference is that joy in God is joy for a purpose that goes beyond our experience. This is important to highlight. Our desire (and fight) for joy in God is not so that we can soften the cushion of our American comforts.[10] The point is not just that we feel better, or that we achieve some enhanced version of ourselves through a divine tack-on. You'll of course find those sorts of messages on the magazine covers that line the grocery store checkout, and it's certainly attractive. The whole industry of "self-help" literature fixates on the word "just," as writer Greg Jackson points out. "It promises that small changes will have big results. The genre [of self-help] implies that your true life is waiting for you behind the superficial inefficiencies and errors of your current life."[11] *All we need are just a few tweaks*, so goes the spiel, and who wouldn't want to try that?

Well, that's not what we're doing here. When it comes to the joy in God we want restored, it's a joy that intends a purpose much bigger than ourselves. Our joy in God is undoubtedly *our joy*, and yet it's a joy purposed to magnify the glory of God and to seek the good of others.

10. "The fight for joy in Christ is not a fight to soften the cushion of Western comforts. It is a fight for strength to live a life of self-sacrificing love" (John Piper, *When I Don't Desire God* (Wheaton, IL: Crossway, 2004), 20.
11. Greg Jackson, "The Inner Life of a Sinking Ship," *The Hedgehog Review* (Fall 2018), 83–91.

MAGNIFYING THE GLORY OF GOD

We all know joy magnifies something. Whenever we see someone who is manifestly happy, we immediately want to know why. *Where is that happiness coming from?* We instinctively know that joy has a cause, a source, and eventually that source becomes the focus, not the joy itself. For example, imagine you're hanging out with a group of friends, and one of them is looking at her phone. Suddenly, she bursts into laughter. It is spontaneous joy, clear as day. What do you do when you see that? You want to see what she sees, of course! You want to go stand beside her and look at whatever it is that she's looking at. Her manifest joy is pointing away from itself to the thing that caused it. The causer of joy is inescapably proclaimed as valuable by our experience of joy.

Our joy in God is the same way, but only more so, because it magnifies the worthiness of God whether anyone else is watching or not. Even if nobody sees it, our joy in God is like an exhibition of his faithfulness. We are making a statement about God with our hearts and behavior: *Yes, God, you are who you say you are. You are worthy of all praise. You are the all-satisfying treasure of my life.* Our joy doesn't stop with the joy itself; it's about where the joy points. Our joy in God magnifies the glory of God. That's the purpose our joy intends, and it's the ultimate purpose of our lives.

SATISFIED IN JESUS

The most important, all-encompassing truth of the universe is that everything exists for the glory of God—which means, ultimately, everything exists to magnify the weightiness and wonder of who God is. That is the resounding theme of the Bible. But we often need to translate the glory of God from an abstract idea to something more real. We shouldn't imagine God's glory as a bright, blinding light that fills the sky. His glory is certainly seen there (see Psalm 19), but the Bible gets more particular. The writer to the Hebrews tells us that Jesus is "the radiance of the glory of God and the exact imprint of his nature" (Heb. 1:3). Paul says that Jesus is the one in whom the "whole fullness of deity dwells bodily" (Col. 2:9). The apostle John writes that "the Word became flesh and dwelt among us, and we have seen his glory" (John 1:14).

Jesus is the most vivid display of who God is, as he himself has said: "Whoever has seen me has seen the Father" (John 14:9). This means, in a deeply personal way, that the glory of God is the person Jesus. And because that is true—*because of who Jesus is*—there is nothing more important or more relevant than that Jesus is real. Our purpose, then, is to experience and show that Jesus is the supreme satisfaction of our souls. That is what it means to magnify the glory of God. That is what joy *is for*. It's the "why" behind our prayer: *God, give me joy again.*

FOR THE GOOD OF OTHERS

We really don't need any other purpose for our joy, but there is more. In God's economy, the vertical always affects the horizontal. Like with the Greatest Commandment—love God, then people—our joy in God glorifies God and then spills over for the good of others. It's another reminder that our joy doesn't end with an isolated experience, but instead we actually become conduits of joy. That's exactly what happened for the churches in Macedonia.

In 2 Corinthians 8, Paul is holding up the Macedonian Christians as a model of radical generosity. They gave financial relief to poverty-stricken Christians even though they themselves were also poor. *How could they do that?* Because of their abundance of joy, as Paul puts it: "For in a severe test of affliction, their abundance of joy and extreme poverty have overflowed in a wealth of generosity" (2 Cor. 8:2). Their joy propelled them into self-sacrificing love, and the aim of love, in its truest sense, is that others also be happy in God (and the more others are happy in God, the more the glory of God is magnified).

David understood that his joy in God had implications for those around him. Immediately after verse 12, after David prayed for God to restore his joy, he says, "Then I will teach transgressors your ways, and sinners will return to you" (Ps. 51:13). David was not just thinking about himself in these petitions. He had not forsaken everyone else in his quest for personal peace, but he wanted others to want what he wanted. He wanted sinners like him, humans like him, to have joy in God, and to ask God for it. *Give me joy again, God, for your glory and for the good of others.*

———•———

God, *open my lips and my mouth will declare your praise*—because you will be praised, with or without me. You don't need my mouth, and you don't need me at all, but you have made me, and I'm here, and I want to get in on the praise you deserve. And God, you know my heart needs to be changed. Please do in me what only you can do—*create in me a clean heart, O God, and renew a right spirit within me.* And whatever comes, wherever you're leading me, be with me today. Please, God, don't leave me. *Cast me not away from your presence, and take not your Holy Spirit from me.* And give me joy again, God. Give me back the joy I've lost, and then more. Make your sun to shine upon me. Make me feel your smiling face. Make me glad in you, for your glory and the good of others. *Restore to me the joy of your salvation and uphold me with a willing spirit.*

CONCLUSION

Another morning, another day, and I'm awake, sitting at my desk. It's still dark outside, at least for the most part—I can see the eastern sky brighten just behind the trees. I have a few moments here in the quiet before my house starts moving, before the coming and going, the conversations, questions, and needs, before the circumstances pile on. Just that thought is enough to make my mind wander, and it often does. Even in the quiet, and maybe mostly in the quiet, I have to fight against distractions. *God, thank you for today.*

It is a calling from God, my being here in this moment.

"Today is the day," as my dad used to say over breakfast. "The day of what?" I would ask every time. "The *day*," he'd say. "The day is here *today*." And that explanation would work for me. I'm not where I used to be, called yesterday, and I'm not yet where I'm headed, called tomorrow, but God has given me today. The sun is rising.

And I don't know what will happen under that sun. In this moment as I'm writing, as the dark gives way to blue and orange, I am staring into an ocean. It is deep and mysterious, and although I've made some plans, the unknown is overcoming. I cannot plan the things that will never happen to me. I cannot have certainty about what I will face. And that makes me feel small—"*O LORD, what is man that you regard him, or the son of man that you think of him?*" (Ps. 144:3). It is right to feel small, to feel weak. Do I have what I need for the needs I don't know?

God knows I don't know.
But he is merciful.

"The steadfast love of the LORD never ceases; his mercies never come to an end; they are new every morning . . ." (Lam. 3:22–23)—*new* and *enough*. God's mercy is what I need the most, and it's what he has promised me in Jesus Christ—*mercy for today*. So in this moment, right now, I turn from all else and walk in that mercy. It is light outside.

Father,

Let me get in on your praise.
Change me from the inside out.
Please don't leave me.
Give me joy again.

In Jesus's name, amen.

ABOUT THE AUTHOR

Jonathan Parnell is the lead pastor of Cities Church in Minneapolis-St.Paul, a church he and his team planted in 2015. He is the Send Network's City Missionary in the Twin Cities, where he also serves as a church planting trainer. He is the author of *Never Settle for Normal: The Proven Path to Significance and Happiness* (2017) and coauthor of *How to Stay Christian in Seminary* (2014). He and his wife, Melissa, live in the Twin Cities with their eight children.